# Better Homes and Gardens®

# HOW TO paint

## JUST ABOUT ANYTHING

Meredith® Books
Des Moines, Iowa

# How To Paint Just About Anything

Editor: **Paula Marshall**
Project Manager/Writer: **Jean Schissel Norman**
Project Designers: **James Cramer, Patty Mohr Kramer**
Associate Design Director: **Som Inthalangsy**
Copy Chief: **Terri Fredrickson**
Publishing Operations Manager: **Karen Schirm**
Senior Editor, Asset and Information Manager: **Phillip Morgan**
Edit and Design Production Coordinator: **Mary Lee Gavin**
Editorial Assistant: **Kaye Chabot**
Book Production Managers: **Pam Kvitne, Marjorie J. Schenkelberg, Rick von Holdt, Mark Weaver**
Contributing Copy Editor: **Amanda Knief**
Contributing Proofreaders: **Heidi Johnson, Beth Lastine, Jeanne LeDoux**
Contributing Photographers: **Gordon Beall, Scott Little, Jay Wilde**
Indexer: **Bev Nightenhelser**

**Meredith₀ Books**
Executive Director, Editorial: **Gregory H. Kayko**
Executive Director, Design: **Matt Strelecki**
Managing Editor: **Amy Tincher-Durik**
Senior Editor/Group Manager: **Vicki Leigh Ingham**
Senior Associate Design Director: **Ken Carlson**
Marketing Product Manager: **Tyler Woods**

Publisher and Editor in Chief: **James D. Blume**
Editorial Director: **Linda Raglan Cunningham**
Executive Director, Sales: **Ken Zagor**
Director, Operations: **George A. Susral**
Director, Production: **Douglas M. Johnston**
Director, Marketing: **Amy Nichols**
Business Director: **Jim Leonard**

Vice President and General Manager: **Douglas J. Guendel**

***Better Homes and Gardens₀* Magazine**
Editor in Chief: **Karol DeWulf Nickell**
Deputy Editor, Home Design: **Oma Blaise Ford**

**Meredith Publishing Group**
President: **Jack Griffin**
Executive Vice President: **Bob Mate**

**Meredith Corporation**
Chairman and Chief Executive Officer: **William T. Kerr**
President and Chief Operating Officer: **Stephen M. Lacy**

In Memoriam: **E.T. Meredith III (1933-2003)**

# Table of Contents

# Starting Out

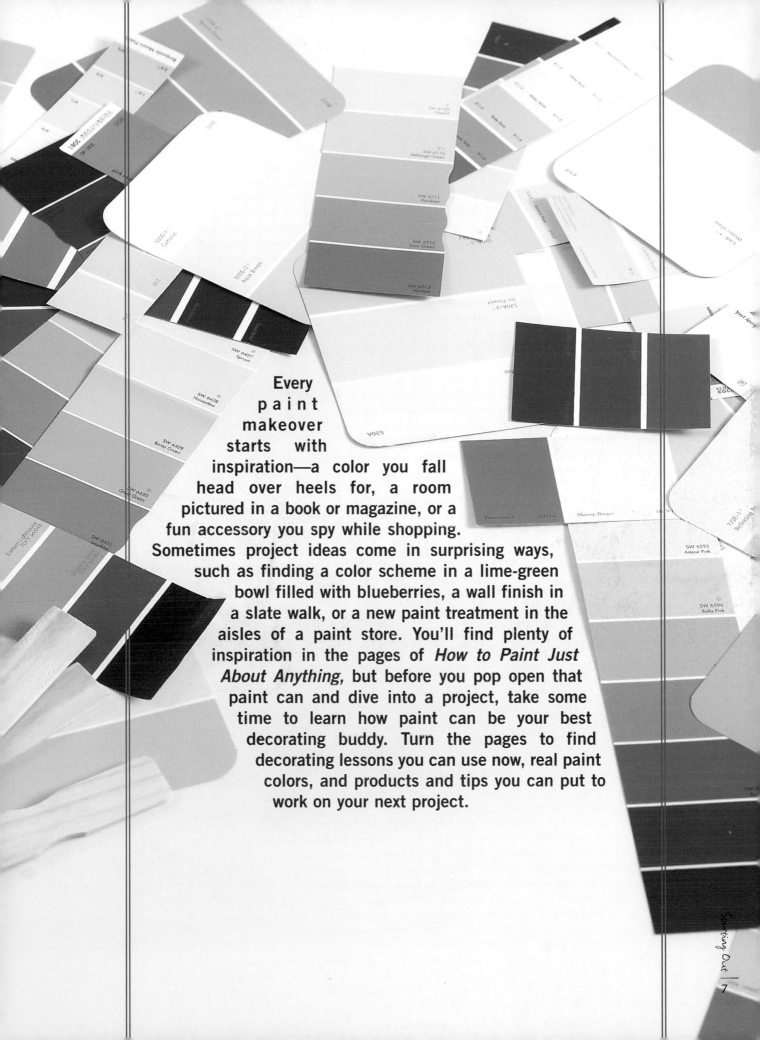

# CHAPTER 1

Every paint makeover starts with inspiration—a color you fall head over heels for, a room pictured in a book or magazine, or a fun accessory you spy while shopping. Sometimes project ideas come in surprising ways, such as finding a color scheme in a lime-green bowl filled with blueberries, a wall finish in a slate walk, or a new paint treatment in the aisles of a paint store. You'll find plenty of inspiration in the pages of *How to Paint Just About Anything,* but before you pop open that paint can and dive into a project, take some time to learn how paint can be your best decorating buddy. Turn the pages to find decorating lessons you can use now, real paint colors, and products and tips you can put to work on your next project.

# What do you know about paint?

You've been painting for years, right? Are your old ways of doing things still the best? Circle your guesses and check out the answers on page 10. More than one answer may be correct for each question.

1. My walls are white, but I want to paint them deep burgundy. How many coats will it take?
A. Two of burgundy.
B. At least four of burgundy.
C. One coat of tinted primer and one or two top coats of burgundy.

2. I hate, hate, hate the pink tiles in my master bathroom. I plan to
A. Start saving for a total redo.
B. Paint them with regular paint and cross my fingers.
C. Use a primer made for glossy surfaces.

3. The woodwork in my house is covered with oil-base paint. I plan to paint it with
A. Latex primer and latex paint.
B. Alkyd or oil-base primer and latex paint.
C. Alkyd or oil-base paint.

4. I'm painting tomorrow and I hate to clean brushes so I'm planning to
A. Buy the cheapest brush and throw it out at the end of the project.
B. Use an old worn brush and toss it when I'm done.
C. Buy a new brush suited to the paint I'm using.

5. I'm not sure which paint color will look good in my kitchen. Should I
A. Buy a gallon and start painting?
B. Buy a quart and test the color on foam-core board?
C. Hold the color swatch up and squint at it to picture it on my walls?

6. I have a mildew problem in my bathroom. What can I do?
A. Paint the walls every year and wash with a bleach solution whenever the mildew appears.
B. Add a mildewcide to paint.
C. Use a paint specially formulated for high-moisture areas such as kitchens and baths.

7. How can I tell if the spots on my basement walls are mildew or dirt?
A. Drop a small amount of bleach on a few of the spots.
B. Scrub the spots with soap.
C. If the spots look like dirt, they are dirt.

8. Isn't alkyd or oil-base paint better than latex paint?
A. Yes.
B. No.
C. It depends.

9. I painted my woodwork with latex paint. Can I paint it with oil now?
A. No.
B. Yes.
C. Maybe.

10. I painted my floors this weekend. The directions say 1 hour drying time. How can I tell when they're ready for traffic?
A. Wait several days.
B. Wait several weeks.
C. Test a hidden spot to see if you can scratch the paint.

11. I want to stencil curtains that need to be washable. What should I use?
A. Any interior paint.
B. Interior paint mixed with a textile medium.
C. Paint made for fabric.

12. My north-facing bedroom always feels cold in winter, but I want it to feel cozy. What color should I paint it?
A. Sky blue.
B. Pumpkin.
C. Apple green.

13. What is the best time of year to paint?
A. Summer.
B. Spring.
C. Fall.
D. Winter.

14. I used painter's tape to edge the woodwork. When do I remove the tape?
A. Sometime within seven days.
B. It doesn't matter.
C. Immediately.

15. The paint color is up and it's just too strong. Any remedies?
A. Start over with a new color of paint.
B. Wash the strong color with a lighter glaze.
C. Learn to live with it.

Paint products aren't what they used to be. Manufacturers spurred on by tougher environmental regulations turned to the laboratory to create paints that are kind to the environment and easy to use. You'll find these new products on the paint shelves along with paint finishes packaged in kits, paints designed to stick tight to slick surfaces, and other finishes that block mildew. It's a fun new world for anyone who loves to paint.

**1.**
C. Primer tinted to the top-coat color is the secret to painting a light wall dark or a dark wall light. Primers have more resins so they provide better coverage.

**2.**
C. Try one of the new primers made specifically for slick surfaces such as ceramic tile. Follow the manufacturer's instructions to ensure a durable surface.

**3.**
A. Use a latex primer after lightly sanding the surface you plan to paint. Top with latex paint.

**4.**
C. Throw out those cheap brushes or use them for something other than painting. A good brush ensures a smooth paint job and sharp edges. Buy the brush to suit the job: synthetic bristles for water-base or alkyd paints and natural bristles for alkyd paints only.

**5.**
B. If you're experienced and have good color sense, you might be able to get by with squinting at a color chip, but most of us need to paint a large sample on foam-core board.

**6.**
B or C. You can add mildewcide, a chemical additive that prevents mildew from growing on paint, or you can use a kitchen/bathroom paint that already includes a mildewcide. Both are formulated to solve your moisture problems, but paint that already contains mildewcide is more effective than adding it yourself. Check paint labels to see if the paint you have chosen contains the additive.

**7.**
A. Drop a small amount of bleach on the suspected mildew. If it's mildew, the spots will lighten. If it's dirt, you won't notice any change. If the spots look like dirt, they might be mildew because it can appear as gray, black, red, or yellow spots.

**8.**
C. Alkyd or oil-base paint once was the preferred paint for its durability, but latex paints have improved so much they've taken over the market. That's because tougher VOC regulations created a climate for improving the technology of water-base coatings.

**9.**
A. Never cover latex with alkyd or oil-base paint. The flexible latex paint will cause the hard oil-base top coat to crack and peel. If you want to use oil-base paint, you'll need to sand the finish and apply the appropriate primer before painting the finish coat.

**10.**
C. There is a difference between dry time, when the paint is ready for light traffic, and cure time, when it's truly durable. It takes several days to weeks for paint to fully cure, depending on the weather. Humidity can keep paint from drying as quickly as the label states. Once paint is completely cured, you should not be able to scratch off the coating.

**11.**
B or C. Use textile medium when you want to paint fabric with interior paint or buy fabric paint at a crafts store. Make sure you follow the directions for application and care. Always test the process on a scrap to make sure you like the feel of the finish.

**12.**
B. A wonderful shade of pumpkin pulled from the warm side of the color wheel will give the room the most warmth. Blue will keep the mood cool.

**13.**
A, B, C, or D. It all depends on where you live. The ideal painting environment is when humidity and temperatures are moderate. Paint dries too slowly in humid weather and can sag. You also run the risk of touching the still-wet surface and leaving a mark. In hot weather, paint dries too quickly to have a chance to level out.

**14.**
C. Remove tape immediately (within an hour) to prevent the paint film from bonding with the wall and the tape. If the paint dries, it will tear when you remove the tape. If you have an area where the paint has dried and the tape is still in place, run a crafts knife along the seam before removing the tape.

**15.**
B. You can do any of the three but one suggestion is to subdue the strong hue with a wash of lighter glaze. Just mix the light glaze with the wall paint and sponge or rag it on the walls.

# How to use this book

Even if your house is overdue for a makeover, you'll no doubt be squeezing the redo between work, ball games, household chores, and more. To simplify the process and help you make good decisions about color, products, and techniques, *How to Paint Just About Anything* is organized by chapters that walk you through the whys and hows of painting. Start here to get the most out of the information that follows:

**1.** Postpone your color decisions until you've read Chapter 2, "Color." You'll be introduced to colors, how they go together, and how they make a space feel. Then look in every chapter and in "Sources" for real paint choices you can use at your house.

**2.** If you're ready to redo a room, turn to the chapter that applies, such as information about painting kitchen surfaces in Chapter 5, "Kitchens & Baths," and advice on creating a cohesive color palette in Chapter 3, "Living & Dining." You'll find color palettes you can copy alongside every room and project. (Just remember that paint colors on the pages of this book may not match manufacturer color chips, so always check out the real color chips before you buy.)

**3.** Each room comes with "Lessons" that provide a quick read about important information, such as why certain paint colors work in a space, how to get a specific finish, and what to consider before buying paint. Think of these lessons as a short course on painting.

**4.** If you're ready to learn more about new finishes or anxious to start a small project, check out the chapters on paint ideas and techniques. This information is in Chapter 4, "Walls," Chapter 6, "Floors," Chapter 8, "Furniture," and Chapter 10, "Accessories." These are full of projects created just for you.

**5.** Learn more about painting every surface in your house by turning to Chapter 12, "Paint Studio." You'll find charts filled with information about painting surfaces, such as concrete, glass, and paneling, as well as simple techniques for painted finishes.

**6.** Ready to roll? Learn the best way to start and finish every painting project in Chapter 12, "Paint Studio."

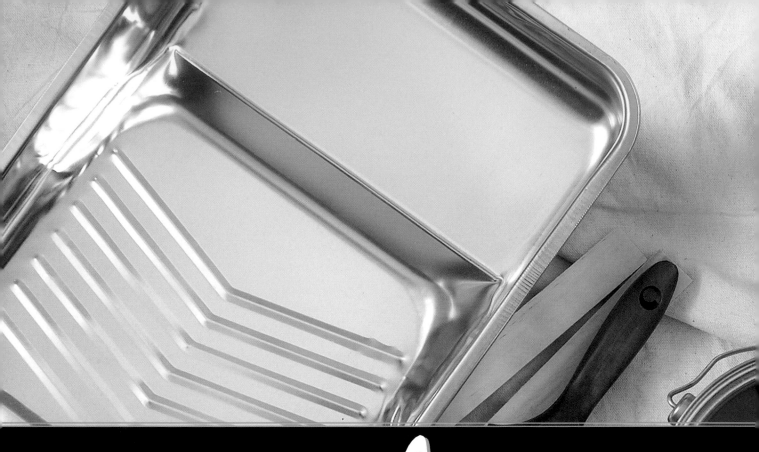

# CHAPTER 2 Color

Paint
by the brushful or the
gallon stands alone as the #1
decorating material. Nothing else offers
as many choices for so little cash. Each just-
opened can promises a fresh beginning. Why
then is it so easy to pick the wrong color, one that's
too harsh or too dull? Why do once-favorite colors
seem dated in just a few months? Why do colors that
look great on a paint chip change color on our walls?
You'll be inspired by the projects shown on these
pages, but before you rush to the store to buy a
gallon or two of spreadable magic, take time to
understand color and its relationship to you and your
home. With an endless number of colors to
consider, an understanding of how color works
will ensure that your paint choices become
long-time favorites. Ready to start? It
begins with the color wheel
shown here.

# Color makes the wheel go round

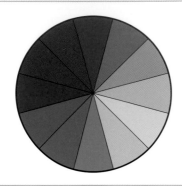

A color wheel is a rainbow in the round, representing the brilliant bars of color that light produces as it passes through a prism. This circular diagram shows relationships between colors. Understanding how color works can simplify the process of picking the perfect hue for your home. Understanding that color is energy makes it easy to comprehend why we respond to it so emotionally. Put these tools together, and you'll be able to pick color palettes that appeal to your eye and your heart.

## PRIMARY COLORS

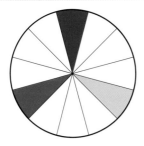

Red, yellow, and blue are pure colors that, when mixed, create every other color on the wheel.

### USE THIS PALETTE

Primary colors are the strongest hues. They provide rooms with brightness and visual bounce. Use them in pairs or combine all three for rooms that feel strong and solid. Mix in neutrals such as white for a crisp look; add black to strengthen the palette. Use tints of primary colors for a soft look and shades for a subdued palette.

### REAL-LIFE PAINT CHOICES:

## SECONDARY COLORS

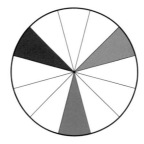

Mixing equal amounts of two primary colors creates secondary colors. Green is made from blue and yellow, orange from yellow and red, and purple from red and blue.

### USE THIS PALETTE

The pairing of two secondary colors results in a lively color scheme. Pick from fall tones of burnt orange and avocado to create a warm scheme. Select green and violet for a palette that mixes warm and cool tones. Pick a tint of one of the colors to ground the scheme.

### REAL-LIFE PAINT CHOICES:

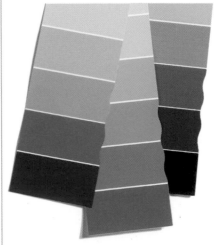

## TERTIARY COLORS

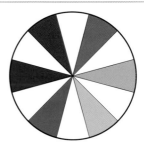

Mixing equal amounts of one primary and either of its secondary colors produces a tertiary color— blue-green, blue-violet, red-violet, red-orange, yellow-orange, and yellow-green.

### USE THIS PALETTE

These colors can be used in schemes that make use of complementary color, (opposites on the color wheel) or analogous colors, (neighbors on the color wheel). The effects they create depend on the pairing, but remember that these blended colors are easier to use in a room scheme than the primary colors from which they evolved.

### REAL-LIFE PAINT CHOICES:

# Color makes a personal statement

To create your personal color palette, collect tear sheets of images that appeal to your sense of color. The tear sheets may show clothing, rooms, food, flowers, etc. Collect the images in a notebook or box. Analyze the color schemes by writing notes, including your emotional reaction to the hues. Then approach the colors scientifically. Are they complementary or analogous? Are they tints or shades? Add these explanations to your notebook. Soon you'll start seeing a pattern. Next time you're shopping for paint, you're more apt to pick color chips that make you feel right at home.

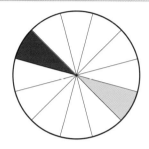

## COMPLEMENTARY COLORS

Opposites on the color wheel, complementary colors partner up to offer maximum contrast with natural balance. Picture a violet flower with its green leaves as an example.

### USE THIS PALETTE

Complementary colors naturally allow warm and cool hues to play off each other, intensifying each color. That means red appears redder and green greener, more so than when each is used alone. To use these color-wheel opposites, make one color the star and provide some air by using a neutral. For the easiest go-together palette, pick soft complementary tones. For a bold look, use deep hues.

### REAL-LIFE PAINT CHOICES:

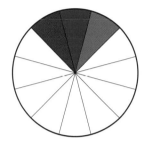

## ANALOGOUS COLORS

What are they? Three hues side by side on the color wheel mix to create a soothing palette.

### USE THIS PALETTE

Neighboring colors are closely related and easy to use together. For this scheme, choose a favorite color for the main hue. Add additional colors from the neighboring hues. For a lively look, vary the intensities of the colors you combine with the dominant hue. Consider, too, creating an analogous scheme that combines warm and cool neighbors on the color wheel.

### REAL-LIFE PAINT CHOICES:

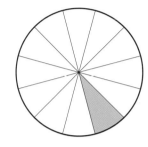

## MONOCHROMATIC COLORS

For an easy scheme, use a single color in a range of value and intensity.

### USE THIS PALETTE

Incorporating variations of a single color can be soothing and sophisticated (cool neutrals) or exciting and vivacious (variations of a hot tropical color). Pick one color and use it in many versions, from tints to shades, for a look that's pulled together. Strong contrasts between lights and darks create energy; subtle variations subdue a mood. For a tranquil scheme, pick a quiet color in all its tones from light to dark. Colors are not competing for attention, so settings are calm.

### REAL-LIFE PAINT CHOICES:

# Working with paint chips

Paint chips are much more than little cards of color. They organize paint collections from a single manufacturer, provide a look at tints and shades of the same color, and help you find coordinating hues. Learn how to talk about color using these common terms. Then put it all together as you study paint cards.

## VALUE

Value is the lightness or darkness of colors. Sky blue is a light value; cobalt is a dark value. Paint chip cards typically have light and dark variations of one color. Use light yellow in one room, for example, and a deeper hue from the same paint-chip card in an adjoining room. For delineation, pick colors separated by at least one chip on a card.

## INTENSITY

This term refers to color saturation and specifies clearness or brightness. Adding white, black, or a complementary color to a pure color diminishes its intensity. To ensure the same intensity for contrasting colors, select hues from the same position on paint chip cards, using the same paint brand.

## TINT

Closest to white in value, tints are also called pastels. You'll find them on the top of a paint card or in a separate collection of whites and off-whites. Tints can appear almost white or stronger in hue.

## SHADE

Darkening or dulling colors with black or gray creates shades. Shades can be near the top of the paint card (think light gray blue) or right at the bottom (deep olive green).

## What the pros know

**Color isn't always what it seems at first blush. Consider the ways color changes once you bring it home.**

• Light changes the perception of color. Paint a sample board the color you are considering. Move the sample board around the room. The look will vary depending on natural light and the type of artificial light as well as whether viewed in the morning or evening.

• Reflections change color. If you live in the woods, the green outdoors will impact how paint "reads" in your house. The color of a nearby building, such as a red brick wall, can add a pink blush to the purest white or turn yellow toward orange.

• Nearby colors affect the look. For example, red looks brighter and larger surrounded by black and duller surrounded by orange.

• Sheen changes color. A flat, matte paint looks darker than the same hue in a glossy finish.

• Texture affects color. Smooth surfaces reflect light and look lighter than a heavily textured wall in the same tone.

# Color and mood

People respond to color with their hearts, not just their heads. The reaction depends on the tint or shade and whether it's warm/active, cool/passive, or neutral. You can easily create a color mood for every room in your house. Here's how:

## WARM/ACTIVE COLORS: RED, YELLOW, AND ORANGE

Extroverts, these advancing hues step out in the room to greet and sometimes dominate. Red, the most intense, pumps the adrenaline like no other hue, stimulating conversation and appetites. Use cheerful yellow to unleash creative juices or to expand small spaces. Orange is the ultimate party color, but it can appeal to everyone depending on the tone, from pumpkin to peach to terra-cotta. Warm colors added to cool colors—yellow to a green scheme or red to a purple palette—can add virtual heat to rooms that feel too cool.

Use these hues when

- Windows are few, so the room lacks natural sunlight.
- Northern exposure admits only cool light.
- Woodsy views create a cool greenish cast.
- Nightlife is the room's main function.
- A stairway or hall in a neutral space would make a great focal point.

## NEUTRAL COLORS: BROWN, BEIGE, GRAY, AND WHITE

These "uncolors" combine and cooperate, bridging different rooms and palettes. They're good transitions on woodwork, trim, and hallways, and in functional spaces such as kitchens and baths. Darker neutrals calm down other colors while light neutrals intensify them.

Use these hues when

- Warm and cool color schemes meet.
- Texture rather than color becomes the decorating star.
- Warm colors feel too bright.
- Cool colors feel too chilly.
- Backgrounds should recede.
- Accent hues change often to follow fashion.

## COOL/PASSIVE COLORS: BLUE, GREEN, AND PURPLE

These cool colors stay quietly in the background to calm and restore and are perfect for bedrooms and private retreats. If you live in a cold climate, add accents of warm colors for warmth and contrast. Blue, although tranquil, can make a room feel chilly. To warm it up, incorporate neutral or warm accents. In dark values, such as eggplant, purple appears sophisticated, and in light values such as lilac it is restful. Green and blue-green reflect the serenity of green grass and a canopy of leaves.

Use these hues when

- Bedrooms and sitting rooms need a tranquil feeling.
- A family room needs to offer serenity.
- A sunny room requires a cool dose of color to keep the room's visual temperature in check.
- Indoors and outdoors meet.
- A bathroom serves as a serene spa.

## COLOR MOOD

Colors create moods. Here's how the experts say they make you feel.

- Pink soothes and promotes affection.
- Yellow expands, cheers, increases energy, grabs attention.
- White energizes and unifies.
- Black strengthens.
- Orange cheers and stimulates appetites and conversation.
- Red stimulates, dramatizes, and competes.
- Green balances and refreshes.
- Purple comforts and creates mystery.
- Blue relaxes, refreshes, and cools.

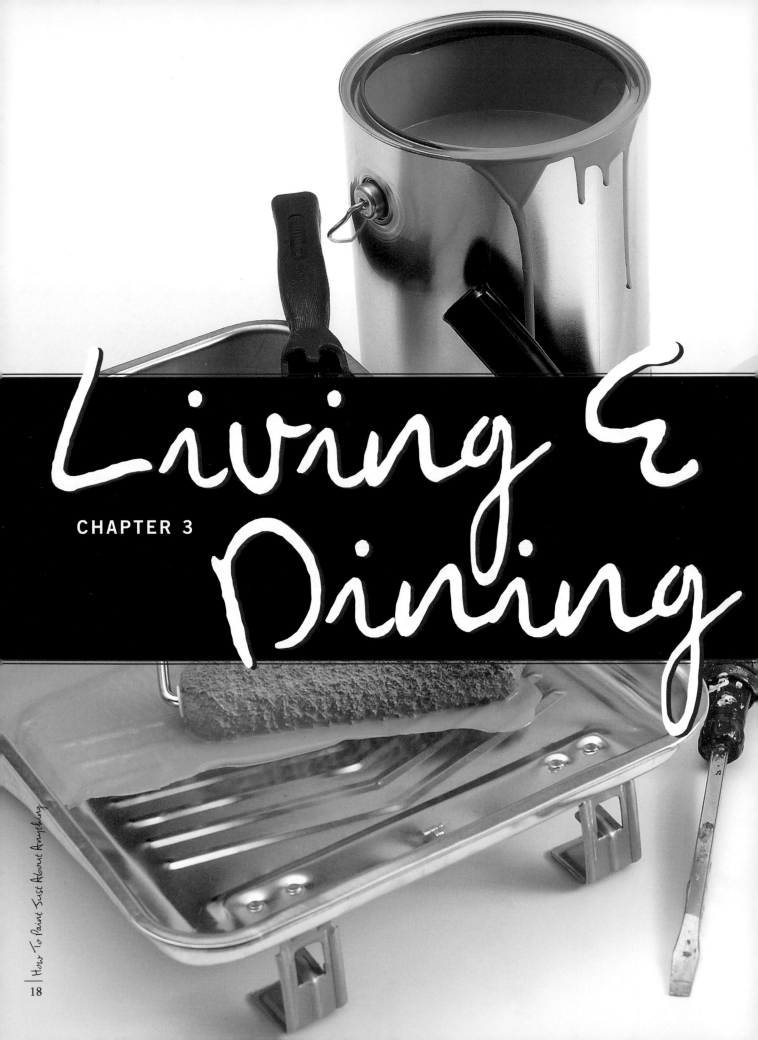

# Living & Dining

They're the spaces that first welcome you home and the rooms where you build memories of shared times with friends and family, but do your living room and dining room really reflect you and your style? Or are you mired in a decorating rut of boring colors and hand-me-down furniture and afraid to take the first step to a fresh new look? Here's help. After all, with a rainbow of colors to choose from and paint products that coat everything from glass to fabric to plaster, you have the raw ingredients at hand for a makeover. And if your taste changes over time, that's no problem. Simply coat the walls or furniture with a stain-blocking primer and spread on a new hue or two.

Check out these painted projects:
• Wood chair frame, page 21
• Vinyl shades, page 22
• Sisal rug, page 27
• Faux wall panels, page 31
• Stenciled fabric, pages 30, 33 and 34
• Glass vases, page 36

Painting the brick white turns this once-dingy fireplace into a focal point. Paints with metal particles add a glow to a flea market frame.

# Grace and age

## THE QUESTION:

*I like the look of old things for my old house. How can I add age to the new pieces I'm bringing home?*

## THE ANSWER:

Try fun techniques and paint products that instantly "age" a new piece. In fact, you'll find that it's time to relax and aim for not-so-perfect in your painting.

## THE LESSONS:

• Start with a neutral color scheme. Soft shades of putty, gray, gold, and oatmeal create a neutral background that pops when mixed with fresh flowers and fun accessories. That flexibility makes a neutral scheme so enduring.

• Matte paint is your friend if you love old things. The good news is that several paint companies have introduced scrubbable matte paints. These no-sheen surfaces hide the imperfections of old plaster walls. For furniture, consider milk paints that offer durability along with low or no sheen.

• Reproduction French chairs sport a finish that starts with deep red paint and includes touches of pink and brown applied randomly with two shades of gold on top. To give the chairs an aged appearance, let the paint dry and then sand it down to raw wood in some places and rough it up using sandpaper, steel wool, and a rasp. To protect the wood, brush on two coats of clear polyurethane in a matte finish.

• New vinyl shades pick up the scrolls of the ironwork outside the window thanks to an oversize stencil (see pages 22–23). To create this project, use painter's tape to make wide stripes on the shade and a stencil for the pattern. If you start with a light-filtering shade, light coming through the shade will show off the texture of the paint. If you want the pattern to appear solid, start with a room-darkening shade and apply two or more coats of paint.

• A brand-new cupboard looks old thanks to a wash of primer, layers of muted tones, and judicious aging with sandpaper and steel wool (see page 23). The idea is to create the look of a cabinet that has been painted and repainted over the years. Apply wear to the cabinet to reflect where hands touched the surface, such as around latches and along outside edges.

• Metallic paints are hotter than ever, reflecting the use of gold, bronze, and silver in fashion. Look for pint-size cans filled with paint that includes real metal, which will tarnish as it ages.

## THE TECHNIQUES:

For more about painting brick, vinyl shades, wood furniture, and fabric, see "Surfaces and how to paint them," starting on page 178.

Vinyl shades, painted with
stripes and stenciled, repeat
the scrollwork outside the
window. The gold on the
shades repeats the color of
the reproduction chairs.

Give a vinyl shade vintage appeal by varying the paint coverage and using a delicate stencil.

Thin paint with textile medium before coating the back of a chair. The stenciled initial adds a personal touch.

A new cabinet looks old with a finish that layers neutral paints, then removes them using sandpaper and steel wool.

## THE PALETTE:

Sources, page 186

TURNING LEAF

METALLIC GOLD

BERKSHIRE GRAY

EDGECOMB GRAY

# High drama

## THE QUESTION:

Help! My new house has high ceilings and wide-open spaces that overwhelm people and furniture. How can I make it more user friendly?

## THE ANSWER:

Add bold scale using paint to create drama that, surprisingly, will bring the space down to size. That might mean a harlequin pattern with diamonds measuring more than 2 feet high on the wall or an oversize metal chandelier painted matte black and hung over the dining room table.

## THE LESSONS:

• In an open space, create a cohesive look with a color palette that flows from one area to the next. For variety and contrast, choose colors that are a step lighter or darker on the paint-chip strip. Temper strong colors, such as citrus yellow and hot pink, with soothing doses of black, white, or brown. In addition to grounding a bright scheme and providing some visual relief, these neutrals lend sophistication.

• Patterns that work in traditional rooms with 8-foot-high ceilings just won't do in houses with vaulted ceilings and few walls. Supersize a standard pattern, such as a harlequin design, to give it enough scale to hold its own in a big space. (Check out www.stencil-library.com for stencil patterns available in three or more sizes.) Black upholstery tacks hammered into the points of the diamonds add even more drama.

• Give old furniture a new look with a coat of satin paint. Distress the painted surface by slightly rubbing the edges with sandpaper or steel wool. Protect the finish with a coat or two of polyurethane unless you want the surface to wear even more.

• Don't forget the small stuff. Lampshades in the entry feature a coat of black paint applied over two coats of multipurpose sealer so the top coat won't bleed through. The circle colors draw from all the hues used in the house. The dining room rug features oversize painted kiwifruit. Use a stencil for the pattern, and coat with acrylic paints.

## THE TECHNIQUES:

For more about painting sisal, see page 91. For painting patterned walls, see "Do the Math" on page 185.

Liberal doses of black and white play up the lime green entrance wall and provide visual relief from the strong color.

The harlequin pattern uses shades of the same color to create a backdrop for fun painted lampshades and flowerpots. Use 2-ounce containers of crafts paint for small projects like these.

*For added drama, kiwifruits fill the corners of an oversize sisal rug. Paint designs freehand or use a purchased stencil.*

*Upholstery tacks add a button of black to the harlequin design.*

## THE PALETTE:

Sources, page 186

**SORCERER**

**TEQUILIA LIME**

**PEAR GREEN**

**MOON RISE**

Bold colors offer a fresh
background for
traditional furniture.
Mix it up by painting
furniture too.

The red and gold upholstery fabric links the gold living room to the red dining room.

It takes only a yard or two of expensive fabric, such as the print used on the pillows, to inspire a color scheme.

# Bold sweep

## THE QUESTION:

*An entry hallway separates my living room and dining room. How can I give each area its own personality while maintaining a cohesive look?*

## THE ANSWER:

Create a palette of analogous colors, such as red-orange, orange, and yellow-orange, that step side by side around the color wheel. Neighboring hues are easy to use and yield a separate yet united color front. Add a complementary color, such as lime green, to give the scheme some design pop.

## THE LESSONS:

• Paints in warm tones can raise the decorating temperature of rooms. The trick is to be bold. Experts suggest you pick the colors you love and then go one step brighter on the paint card. When you're creating a bright color scheme that flows from room to room, paint big pieces of foam-core board and set them so you can see all the hues in one viewing.

• Start painting the central hallway first so you can paint walls in adjacent rooms and slowly build your decorating palette.

• Not sure where to start with color? Find a fabric you love and select colors that coordinate. The pillows in tangerine, lime green, red, and gold inspired this color selection. That doesn't mean that every color matches the tones of the pillow fabric. Instead, shades on the walls blend with the fabric.

• Don't forget the furniture. Wood pieces provide the perfect venue for your scheme and let you introduce colors that complement the wall paints.

## THE TECHNIQUES:

For more about painting wood and walls, see "Surfaces and how to paint them," starting on page 178.

## THE PALETTE:

Sources, page 186

**SUNPORCH**

**ORANGE GROVE**

**APRICOT FLOWER**

# revving up neutrals

## THE QUESTION:

My furniture is neutral and so are my walls. I just want some color in my life. What changes can I make without spending a fortune?

## THE ANSWER:

That's an easy one. A gallon of paint in any color should cover the walls in a small room. A quart of two colors can provide the accents, including painted "panels," a pillow, and a window shade that make use of what you already own. A single paint pen can add the final flourish to chair backs. A stencil provides all the pattern you'll need.

## THE LESSONS:

• Paint offers the best choice for a makeover that's high on style and low on cost. When you start with basic neutrals such as a white slipcover, a sisal rug, and a painted sideboard, it's easy to add color. If you've been living with neutrals for a long time, start slowly by adding just one hue, such as this pretty blue.

• Create painted "panels" by layering white paint over the blue walls. To create this look, divide the wall into equal-size sections, allowing spaces between panels. To paint the panels, pencil marks on the walls to indicate the edges of the panels, align a level with the pencil marks, then draw a paintbrush along—but not touching—the level. The painted lines will vary in thickness and paint coverage. Practice this technique on a sample board. For crisp lines, use the level to draw light pencil lines on the walls indicating the inside and outside of each stripe; adhere painter's tape to both penciled lines. Burnish the edges of the tape so the paint won't bleed under it. Paint using a roller or sponge brush. Carefully remove the tape before the paint dries.

• To make a stripe on a round object such as a lampshade, use stretchable automotive tape. Buy the tape in the width of the stripe you want. Place a row of tape along the bottom edge of the shade, a second row of tape adjacent to the first, and a third row of tape adjacent to the second. Remove the middle row of tape; paint.

• For fabric accessories, use paint one or two shades darker than the wall tone. The same color looks light when stenciled on a charcoal denim pillow and dark stenciled on a white linen shade. For both projects, thin the paint with textile medium and apply it using a foam roller.

• Outlined numbers add a custom look to discount chairs. Use a paint pen instead of needle and thread to create the look of stitched numbers on chair backs.

## THE TECHNIQUES:

For more about stenciling on fabric, see page 183.

Misty blue splashes
style on this formerly
neutral living space.
Hand-painted lines
create wall panels.

Whether store-bought or sewn at home, pillows are perfect canvases for stenciling. Make sure you add a textile medium to the paint to ensure easy care.

Outline the painted panels by drawing a loaded artist's brush along the side of a spirit level.

Imperfections in the new painted panels complement the worn surfaces of the old painted sideboard.

How To Paint Just About Anything

Make the most of a stencil pattern by applying it to a flat fabric panel that shows off every detail. Line the shade to make the pattern stand out day and night. Leave it unlined to let the sun filter through.

A stripe of blue adds style to a basic lampshade.

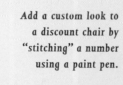

Add a custom look to a discount chair by "stitching" a number using a paint pen.

## THE PALETTE:

Sources, page 186

KIWI SPLASH TURQUOISE MIST

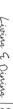

# The S-Curves

## THE QUESTION:

The dining room in my rowhouse is low on natural light. I'd like it to feel bright even without the lights on. Is there any solution?

## THE ANSWER:

Bring the light back into the room by creating some of your own with a sunny color, such as yellow-green, banded by bright white. Add pattern by painting curlicues with semigloss paint that glows even in low light.

## THE LESSONS:

• Start your color scheme by playing off what's already there. The heart-pine floors in this room cast a rosy glow, so complement them with green, its opposite on the color wheel. These complementary schemes offer maximum contrast with natural balance. Imagine a pink flower with spring green leaves. That's why two shades of pink—neighbors on a paint-chip strip and in the adjacent hallway—create the perfect partnership with green.

• Add subtle pattern to the walls. The curlicue S appears and disappears as you walk through the room. A paint pen provides an easy vehicle for delivering dashes of white in semigloss paint. Because the room is painted in a scrubbable matte paint, the glossy sheen of the S shows up in even low light. It's best to create the pattern on a floor-to-ceiling piece of paper, then temporarily adhere the pattern to the wall. Follow the pattern to create dashes of paint that look hand-painted and irregular.

• Create even more shimmer by painting inexpensive glass bottles and vases with gray and silver glass paint. Grouped on the mantel, they offer added impact whether filled with fresh flowers or empty. Gather a variety of sizes and shapes to create this fun collection.

• Dress up a plain table with a tablecloth you paint yourself. Start with a purchased table round, then use a stencil to randomly add flowers using acrylic paint thinned with textile medium. This tablecloth features two shades of pink for the petals. Use a metallic paint pen to deliver the final flourish—a squiggle around the center of each flower. Using a paint pen is as simple as using a marker.

## THE TECHNIQUES:

For more about painting special finishes, see "Special Paint Techniques," starting on page 182.

Try this updated stencil technique using a paint pen to make white dashes that follow the lines of a stencil.

Turn an assortment
of clear vases into a
collection using paints
suitable for glass
and massing them
on a mantel.

*How To Paint Just About Anything*

Curlicues made using a paint pen create a hand-painted wall finish. The glossy white paint reflects light more than the matte wall color.

Mix acrylic crafts paint with a textile medium before using it on fabric so you can launder the finished project. Add a paint-pen squiggle.

When painting glass, cover up the areas you want to remain clear and paint everything else with several light coats.

## THE PALETTE:
Sources, page 186

**ARTICHOKE HEARTS**

**FROSTED GLASS**

**HYDRANGEA FLOWER**

**DELICATE ROSE**

The pattern painted on the walls was inspired by an 18th-century chinoiserie pattern and mimics the curves of the crystal chandelier.

# Fine dining

## THE QUESTION:

*I love to entertain, but I'm more apt to invite my guests to the patio dining area than to my boring all-white dining room. Any ideas?*

## THE ANSWER:

Color and pattern can lift any room out of the decorating doldrums. Try this idea: Combine bold yellow-gold with a dramatic flourish of white. Although these walls were hand-painted, you can create a similar look with stencils.

## THE LESSONS:

• Be bold with color in a large room. The yellow-gold adds drama surrounded by white and wood tones. Create the look of wainscoting with paint by dividing the height of the room into fifths and painting the lower two-fifths white. Make sure the color you select looks good in sunshine and candlelight. To do that, paint a piece of foam-core board with the color you love and view it in the room morning, noon, and night.

• Think beyond standard stencil techniques. Instead of using one pattern, combine several. Look for a border pattern to create the rectangular framework, added embellishments for the top center and corners, and an allover design for the center of the focal point wall. (Use an online search engine to find chinoiserie stencil patterns that duplicate this look.) Keep the palette simple by using white as a dramatic counterpoint to the background. When using stencils, temporarily adhere them to the walls using stencil adhesive, then use brushstrokes instead of dabbing in the cutout portions of the stencils to lend a hand-painted look.

## THE TECHNIQUES:

For more about painting with stencils, see "Special Paint Techniques," on page 183.

## THE PALETTE:

Sources, page 186

BUTTERCORN      SQUASH

CHAPTER 4 *Walls*

So many walls and so little time. It's why you'll love the paint treatments featured in this chapter. Many paint products come packaged in kits that offer easy directions and everything you need from start to fancy finish. Many of these wall treatments can be problem-solvers as well. Rough walls? Try a stone or suede finish. Their minimal sheen and added texture disguise imperfections. Boring walls? Rev up the style with a finish that looks like fabric or try a paint-by-number mural your child will love. Both finishes are geared for amateurs yet yield professional-looking results. The only problem? You probably can't use all of these finishes in the same house.

Try a fun paint technique:
- Canvas, page 42
- Stone, page 44
- Suede, page 46
- Venetian plaster, page 50
- Color wash and stencil, page 52

# Canvas

## THE QUESTION:

*I've noticed painted treatments that look like fabric. I would love to copy this look for my bedroom walls. Can I really complete a room in a weekend?*

## THE ANSWER:

You'll be pleasantly surprised how easy paint manufacturers make this type of technique. In fact, you can purchase everything you need in one kit. But before you make the leap, check online. Many paint manufacturers provide step-by-step photographs and videos of the process. It's more fun and efficient to create this painted finish with a partner. One person can roll on the glaze; the other can make horizontal and vertical passes with the brush.

## THE TECHNIQUE:

Use a kit to create the finish or buy the materials—paint, glaze, and brush—separately so you can use any paint color.

1. Prepare the wall by painting it with white semigloss paint; let dry. Divide the wall into vertical panels no more than 42-inches wide using a level and a colored pencil that matches the final coat. Tape off every other panel; apply glaze to one panel at a time.

2. For the glaze step, roll glaze over the entire surface of one panel (photo A). Because the glaze dries in 20 minutes, it's important to work quickly. Start by dragging a canvas brush horizontally across the panel from one side to the other; repeat in the opposite direction. Wipe the brush tips on a rag after every other pass. After completing the horizontal pattern, drag the brush through the glaze vertically from top to bottom without lifting the brush from the wall (photo B). Repeat until the section is done. The vertical and horizontal brush marks duplicate fabric weave marks. Remove tape; let dry overnight. Tape off remaining panels and repeat the process.

## THE PALETTE:

Sources, page 186

### MORNING PINK

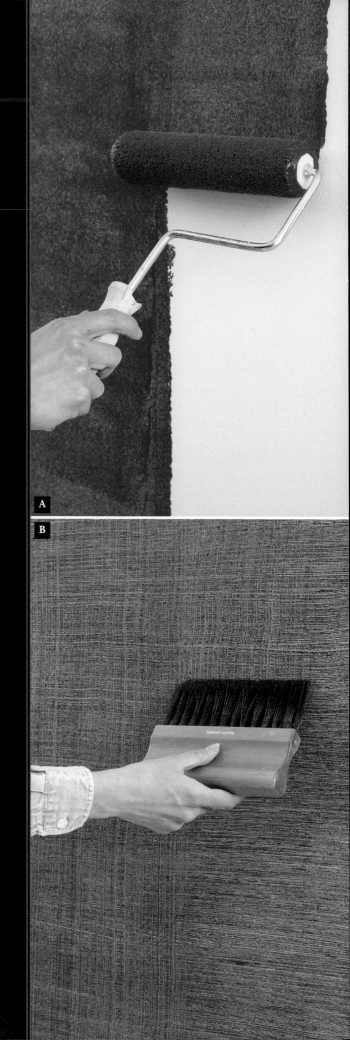

A

B

Use vertical and
horizontal brush-
strokes to mimic
the weave of fabric.

Textured finishes hide
wall imperfections
with a matte finish
and subtle shading.

**A**

## THE QUESTION:

The walls in my attic bedroom are cracked, dented, and worn. Is there anything I can do to cover up the mess short of hanging new drywall?

## THE ANSWER:

A paint finish with the look and texture of stone can cover up rough wall areas and make cracks and dents look like they are part of the design.

## THE TECHNIQUE:

1. No need to repaint walls to start unless the existing wall color is bold. Protect woodwork with painter's tape and flooring with a leak-proof drop cloth; mask corners to prevent double coverage. Use a thick-nap roller cover to roll the textured stone product onto the wall, leaving some areas thicker and some thinner. Coat corners and areas too small for the roller using a trim brush. Cover the wall in sections of only about 4×4 feet at a time.

2. Smooth the textured stone with a trowel or drywall mudding tool. (You can find these tools at home improvement stores.) The trick to smoothing the finish is to develop a consistent technique and work one wall at a time. After completing the first wall, work the opposite wall, then the walls in between. Allow the finish to dry overnight before applying glazes. A partner simplifies the process because one person can roll on the stone treatment and the other can smooth the finish.

3. Most finishes make use of two glazes, one light and one dark, to give a realistic look to the finish. Let the first glaze dry before applying the top glaze. Pour a small amount of the glaze onto a plate. Dip a lint-free rag into the glaze and apply it to the wall in a circular motion (photo A). Use a trim brush to apply glaze to areas along the ceiling or woodwork but immediately soften brush marks with a rag. Work one wall at a time before the glaze dries.

## THE PALETTE:

Sources, page 186

TAUPE

MOCHA

# Suede

## THE QUESTION:

Can I create a suede look for our home office that's more than a solid textured wall?

## THE ANSWER:

Suede finishes are so easy to work with you can have some fun and create a checkerboard wainscot.

## THE TECHNIQUE:

1. Suede walls create a warm background in a family room or home office. To bring the look of this sample panel to your house, divide your wall into upper and lower sections by marking a level horizontal line 44 inches from the floor. Apply 2-inch-wide painter's tape below the horizontal line; this area will be covered by chair rail.

2. On the upper wall, apply three colors of suede paint in a crosshatch motion using a 2- to 3-inch trim brush. Using two or three colors adds dimension to the wall. If you can't find the exact color you want, feel free to mix colors. This works particularly well when you mix two shades of green, for example, to get a midrange color. Use the same brush for all colors, dipping into the color and crosshatching as quickly as possible from top to bottom. Remove tape; let dry.

3. For the lower wall, roll on the first coat of suede paint in a vertical motion, remove tape, and let dry. To create the blocks, use a level and pencil to mark three horizontal lines every 11 inches and vertical lines every 16 inches. Before painting, apply painter's tape around the perimeter of each block (photo A). Create a checkerboard pattern by painting every other block with a second color, using a crosshatch motion (photo B). Remove tape.

## THE PALETTE:

Sources, page 186

**SHADOW RIDGE**

**DESERT CACTUS**

**TALLGRASS PRAIRIE**

Combine two or
three paint colors
for a finish that
looks like suede.

Special paints let you
cover up old ceramic
tile right on the wall.

How To Paint Just About Anything

# Ceramic tile

## THE QUESTION:

The ceramic tile in my bathroom is in good shape, but I don't like the color. Can I really paint it?

## THE ANSWER:

There's more than one way to paint ceramic tile. Binding primers provide the tooth for a top coat of paint while special paints for slick surfaces can also provide a new surface. Here's one way to get the job done.

## THE TECHNIQUE:

1. Clean tile thoroughly with a nonsoapy detergent and let dry. Remove any surface residue with denatured alcohol.

2. Paint the lower section of the tile wall using special enamel crafts paint. Squirt a couple of tablespoons of the paint onto a ceramic dish and apply paint using a 2- to 2½-inch trim brush to a masked-off section no more than 3×3 feet. Immediately lay plastic wrap over the painted surface, pressing the wrap flat to the tile with the palm of your hand. Do not run fingers over plastic wrap because streaks can appear. Remove plastic wrap, then pounce a ball of plastic wrap on the surface to remove more glaze as desired. Touch up as necessary while the paint is still tacky. Allow each section to dry thoroughly before moving painter's tape and completing another section.

3. Using painter's tape, protect the border area using the tile as a straightedge. Squirt a couple of tablespoons of a second paint color onto a ceramic plate. Using a 2- to 2½-inch trim brush, paint a two-foot-long border area of tile and grout (photo A). Follow process used above to create texture using plastic wrap (photo B). Let paint dry for 21 days before cleaning.

## THE PALETTE:

Sources, page 186

**HYDRANGEA**          **FRESH FOLIAGE**

# Venetian plaster

## THE QUESTION:

A home show in my area included family room walls surfaced with a smooth, almost shiny, plaster finish. They called it Venetian plaster. Can I apply that finish over my painted drywall?

## THE ANSWER:

This popular finish is available from several paint companies. It's perfect for giving standard drywall a custom finish, and it can cover up wall imperfections.

## THE TECHNIQUE:

1. Mask off woodwork and protect flooring with waterproof drop cloths. Apply a medium-color base coat to your walls; let dry. Add the first, thin layer of colored Venetian plaster, working with a 4- to 5-inch trowel. Hold the trowel at a 15- to 30-degree angle and apply the plaster in a crosshatch motion (photo A). Let plaster dry.

2. Holding the trowel at a 60- to 90-degree angle, apply a second thin layer of Venetian Plaster. Let dry overnight.

3. Within seven days, burnish the plaster using very fine 400- to 600- grit sandpaper (photo B). Wipe off plaster dust; burnish with the flat side of a trowel if desired. This last burnishing step adds luster to the raised areas of the Venetian plaster.

## THE PALETTE:

Sources, page 186

**SHALE GRAY**

**AMALFI COAST**

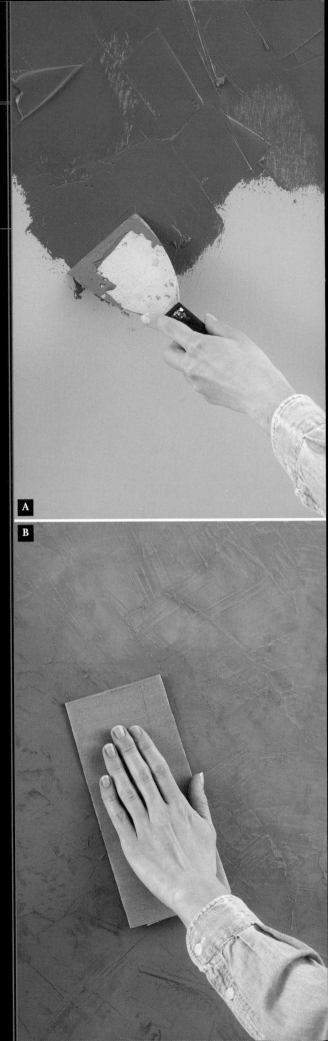

A

B

*A Venetian plaster finish lends a hand-troweled look to drywall.*

Be playful and combine
wall finishes, such as
this color wash layered
with stencils.

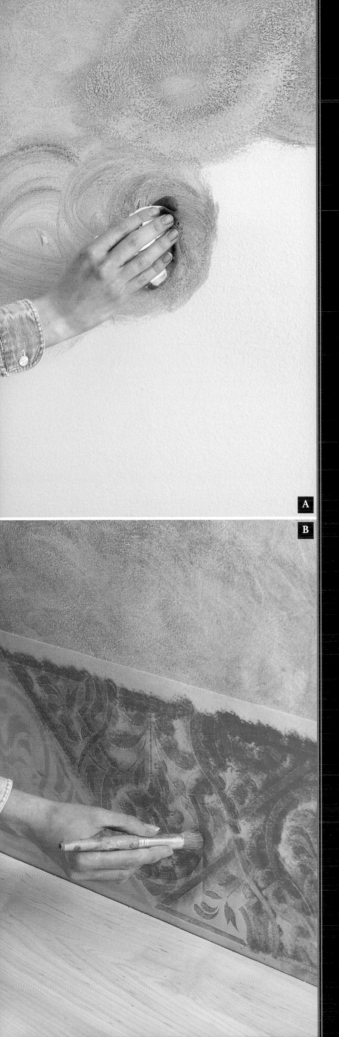

# Color wash/stencil

## THE QUESTION:

*I sponged my walls years ago. Now I've noticed a subtler wall finish that looks almost like watercolor sponging. What is this technique?*

## THE ANSWER:

The soft finish you noticed is called color wash. It makes use of a soft rag rather than a sponge to apply a mix of paint and water. Not only does it offer a softer look than sponging, it's also a great background for stencils and stamps. Look for this product under many brand names.

## THE TECHNIQUE:

1. Begin with a white wall in a satin sheen. The satin finish allows the paint to move on the surface rather than soaking into the paint. If your walls are already painted white, you need not repaint. Mask off ceiling, corners, and molding.

2. To make the wash, mix equal parts of water and colored wash in a bucket. Working quickly, apply the wash to the walls with a rag, working from top to bottom in large circles (photo A). Use a brush to apply wash near the ceiling; soften brush marks with the rag. Keep the circles irregular like puzzle pieces rather than making square sections. Finish one wall before beginning another; let paint dry. Repeat on all other walls to be washed.

3. Repeat the process with a second layer of the same color. Let dry overnight. Mix a second color wash of equal parts water and colored wash. Add one layer of this wash over the previous wash; let dry overnight. Layering colors of wash provides a more interesting finish.

4. Stencil a double border at the base of the wall. To stencil, spray the back of the stencil with stencil adhesive. Press the stencil in place, and apply paint using a stencil brush and an up-and-down motion. This project used a 3:1 mix of russet and metallic copper paints. Begin stenciling with a medium-size stencil brush (photo B). Finish the first border; then add another border above, lining up the stencil to make a mirror image of the bottom border. When stenciling over color-washed walls, vary the amount of paint applied so the finished effect looks aged to match the washed finish.

## THE PALETTE:

Sources, page 186

MOROCCAN RED

CURRY

# Art for the walls

## THE QUESTION:

I'm not an artist, but I would love to paint a mural on the walls of my child's bedroom. Is there an easy way for an amateur painter like me to create a mural?

## THE ANSWER:

Remember those paint-by-number creations you made when you were a kid? Get out your paintbrushes and paint pens for a grown-up version that lets you turn any wall—in a kid's bedroom or playroom—into an art project.

## THE TECHNIQUE:

1. Start with a mural kit. This project used a kit from one manufacturer and made adaptations to the pattern to suit this space. To give the mural your personal touch, feel free to eliminate parts of the pattern or to duplicate extra elements, such as the stars, and spread them around the walls.

2. Paint the walls a base coat in washable satin finish; use painter's tape to secure the mural pattern and transfer paper (blue side down) to the wall. Trace the pattern using an ink pen (photo A). Lift up a corner of the paper to make sure the blue is transferring to the wall. Remove pattern and transfer paper.

3. Cover blue pattern lines using a black paint pen with a medium tip. Fill in the spaces between black lines using a small brush and acrylic crafts paint (photo B). Don't worry if the paint covers some of the black lines. Just retrace all the outlines with the black paint pen.

## THE PALETTE:

Sources, page 186

**SPA**

**JUBILEE GREEN**

**LISA PINK**

**PASSION**

**CRICKET**

**PUMPKIN**

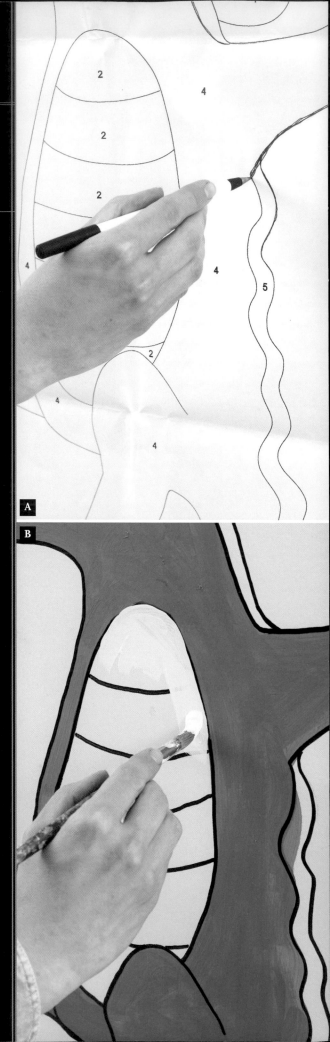

A

B

Paint-by-number wall murals add personality to any wall. When you're ready for a new look, simply cover up the mural with a coat of stain-blocking primer.

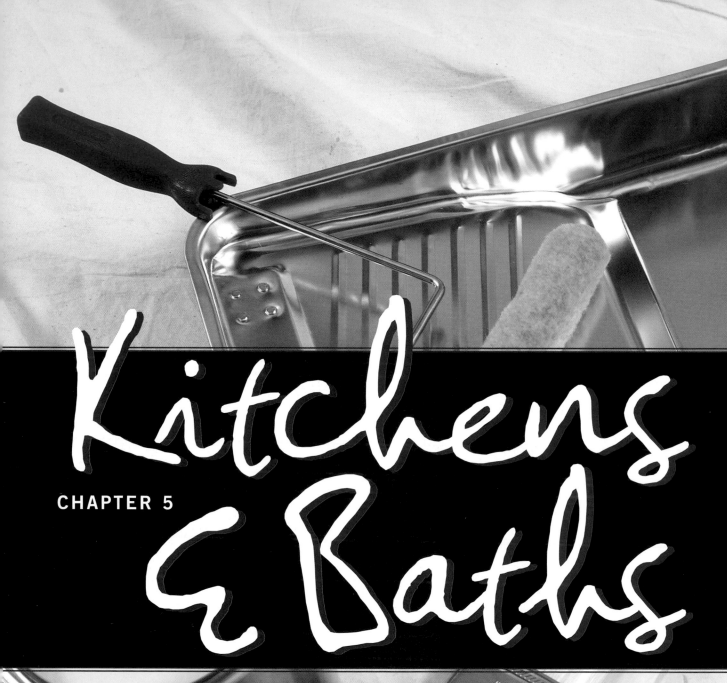

# Kitchens & Baths

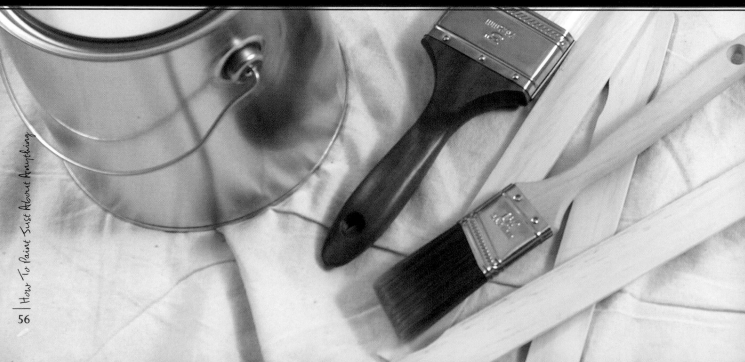

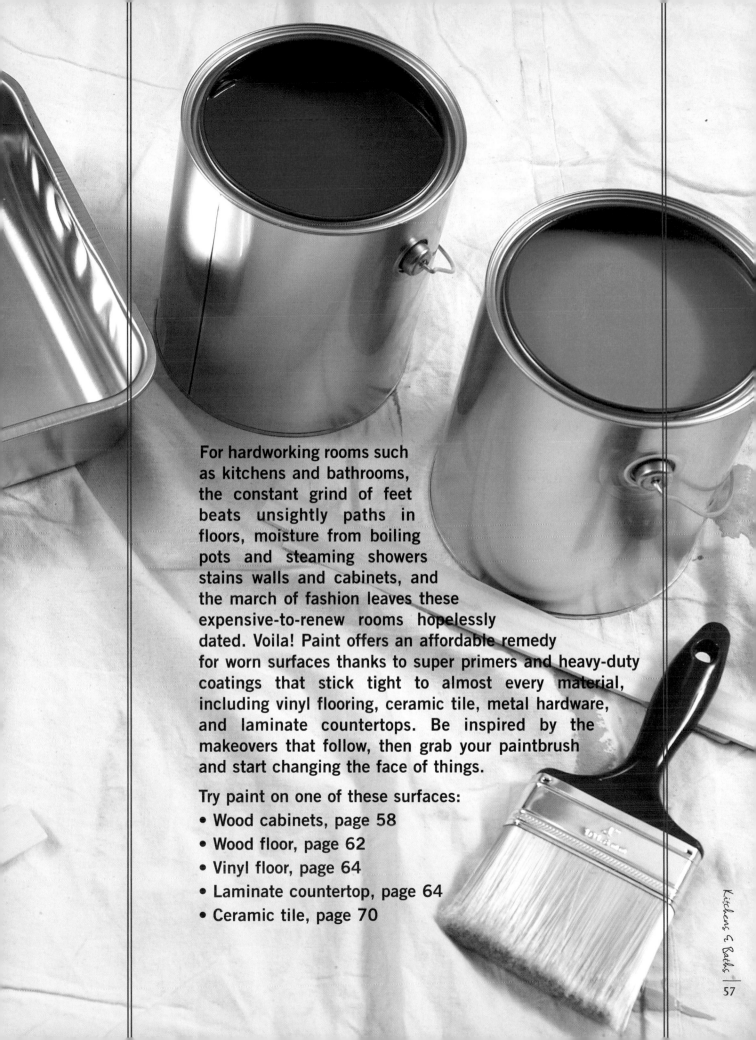

For hardworking rooms such as kitchens and bathrooms, the constant grind of feet beats unsightly paths in floors, moisture from boiling pots and steaming showers stains walls and cabinets, and the march of fashion leaves these expensive-to-renew rooms hopelessly dated. Voila! Paint offers an affordable remedy for worn surfaces thanks to super primers and heavy-duty coatings that stick tight to almost every material, including vinyl flooring, ceramic tile, metal hardware, and laminate countertops. Be inspired by the makeovers that follow, then grab your paintbrush and start changing the face of things.

Try paint on one of these surfaces:
- Wood cabinets, page 58
- Wood floor, page 62
- Vinyl floor, page 64
- Laminate countertop, page 64
- Ceramic tile, page 70

Once an all-white kitchen, this space now sports a colorful outlook using a pretty palette on cabinetry, walls, and floors.

How To Paint Just About Anything

# Spring thaw

## THE QUESTION:

Our all-white kitchen is too new to remodel but it feels cold and clinical. How can we make it the center of cozy family living?

## THE ANSWER:

Generate warmth with paint in a happy spring palette of apple green, lemon yellow, watery blue, and denim blue. These colors, a mix of warm and cool, raise the decorating temperature and divide a big kitchen into the perfectly colored sum of its parts.

## THE LESSONS:

• Juggle a variety of colors in one space by picking a similar midrange intensity. Paint chips that show the range of a hue from light to dark direct you to similar intensities. The color at the top of one card should be of the same intensity as the color at the top of another card. The colors for this kitchen come from the center of the paint cards.

• Structure the color scheme by opting for blocks of one color in specific areas. This trick makes a large kitchen feel smaller and creates the effect of an unfitted kitchen, a style that's common in England. The butler's pantry wears yellow while the island sports the brightest shade: apple green. Upper and lower cabinets are painted two shades of blue.

• Add oomph to your color scheme with painted finishes. Translucent glazes, decorative stippling, and dry-brush painting techniques help strong colors work together. The blue cabinets feature a dry-brush dragged finish while the yellow cabinetry was lightly stippled. A green-gold glaze quiets the vibrant green of the island.

• Be brave and paint stained wood floors for a fitting footnote. Because this room is large, the scale of the floor squares—12 inches—suits the space. The two shades of green play off the darker shade of the island and ensure that the island remains the focal point. Creating a floor like this involves a lot of measuring and taping but the actual painting is simple. Some experts suggest painting the floor in durable alkyd paint; others recommend using latex paint and protecting the finish with at least two coats of polyurethane.

## THE TECHNIQUES:

For more about painting surfaces, see "Surfaces and how to paint them," beginning on page 178.

Two shades of blue add interest to the cabinets. A wash of cream-white glaze, dragged over the painted surface, subdues the clear blues. Painted floors provide the largest pattern in the room.

How To Paint Just About Anything

Bright yellow paint on cabinetry in the butler's pantry works with the kitchen hues.

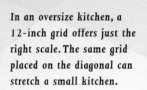

In an oversize kitchen, a 12-inch grid offers just the right scale. The same grid placed on the diagonal can stretch a small kitchen.

Left:

A green-gold glaze subdued the bright apple green of the island; random sanding added the right touch of age to the painted doors.

## THE PALETTE:

Sources, page 186

**KEY LIME**

**CHILLED LEMONADE**

**SOAR**

**FRESH WATER**

# Floor note

## THE QUESTION:

Our kitchen and breakfast room are all white with wood floors. I would like to add some color but I like my white cabinets. Any ideas?

## THE ANSWER:

Here's an idea you're sure to love. Paint the floors. It might seem crazy until you see the powerful impact of a painted floor with an lively stencil repeat.

## THE LESSONS:

• Looking for a color scheme you can live with? Start by searching through the cupboards around your house. The color scheme of this kitchen was inspired by the homeowners' collection of blue and white china. Fresh green paint for the breakfast room walls adds a color twist. A bit of the green even falls to the floor as an occasional leaf stencil.

• Turn the floor into the focal point of the room with this paint treatment. Before you start, paint a large piece of foam-core board to look like the final effect you imagine. Live with the painted piece on the floor to make sure you'll be happy with the effect. Take care to select products suitable for the hard use of a kitchen. Possibilities include a high-quality primer topped with floor enamel; or a high-quality primer, standard latex paint, and two or more coats of clear polyurethane to protect the paint finish. The second option might be the best combination of products when you plan to add a decorative element, such as a stencil, to the floor. Keep in mind that you'll need to recoat the floor every year or two with polyurethane.

## THE TECHNIQUES:

For more about painting cabinets and floors, see "Surfaces and how to paint them," beginning on page 178.

## THE PALETTE:

Sources, page 186

**BLUEBIRD**

**SPARKLING BROOK**

**COMMON LARCH GREEN**

**BLUE HOUR**

Opposite bottom:
*A painted oak floor with stenciled oak leaves, acorns, and whimsical polka dots is the "wow" factor in this kitchen redo.*

Left:
*Green paint adds a splash of color to the breakfast area. A trendy color such as this freshens up a traditional blue and white color scheme.*

Above:
*Crisp white painted cabinetry suits the era of the house and lets the floor take center stage.*

Neutral tones cover up
every surface in this
once-dated kitchen.

How To Paint Just About Anything

# Biding time

## THE QUESTION:

*We just bought a new house, and the kitchen looks terrible. We need to put off remodeling for a few years while we tackle other projects. Is there any way to make this room look better while we wait?*

## THE ANSWER:

Paint lets you clean up your kitchen without soaking your budget. Consider paint for walls, countertops, cabinetry, vinyl flooring, radiators, and even the window treatments.

## THE LESSONS:

• Compose a sophisticated color palette of gray, cream, and shiny stainless steel when your kitchen is hopelessly outdated. Too much color and pattern might call attention to flaws rather than obscure them. When using neutral hues, add interest by combining sheens, such as semigloss with matte paint. Consider paints with texture, such as hammered metal, to provide even more variety.

• Pick from fashion-forward colors when it's time to add accessories. The yellow-green hue used here adds a bold note to the painted vinyl shade. To paint the vinyl shades, use painter's tape to create the stripe; roll on semigloss latex paint using a 4-inch foam roller.

• Cover up kitchen surfaces with a fresh coat of color. Always test products in a hidden area before painting. The laminate countertop now sports a new shade of charcoal that mimics the look of slate. Vinyl flooring, once aged and yellowed, looks fresh again with a coat of cream paint topped with a damask stencil in soft gray and protected with three coats of clear polyurethane. The stencil creates wide stripes across the narrow room. If you're painting over vinyl, work with the imprinted pattern to yield the best results. Stainless-steel cabinet pulls and self-leveling paint update the worn wood base cabinets; the upper cabinets were removed to open up the tiny kitchen.

## THE TECHNIQUES:

For more about painting vinyl floors and laminate countertops, see "Surfaces and how to paint them," beginning on page 178.

This fool-the-eye kitchen makeover includes laminate countertops painted to look like slate and vinyl flooring stenciled to look like damask.

Bold painted stripes on an inexpensive vinyl shade make it a focal point.

Dated laminate hides under a coat of charcoal paint. Even the cake stand sports painted stripes.

Worn vinyl flooring looks brand new thanks to a painted finish that includes a damask pattern stenciled in stripes.

## THE PALETTE:
Sources, page 186

WINTER CALM

FRENCH CANVAS

OBSIDIAN GLASS

TURNING LEAF

REVERE PEWTER

# Heart of the home

## THE QUESTION:

*Our kitchen is already family central so I'd like to use chalkboard paint to make it even harder working as our communications center. Where can I use this paint?*

## THE ANSWER:

Great idea! Chalkboard paint comes in brush-on and spray forms, so it's easy to apply to almost any surface. Try some of these fun ideas for getting the message across.

## THE LESSONS:

• Chalkboard paint comes in schoolhouse green and chalky black. It's easiest to pick a color palette that lets the chalkboard paint star, such as this sage green and butter-yellow scheme. Add a splash of red for accent.

• Plan chalkboards for various uses and spread them throughout the kitchen. A large painted section near the breakfast area makes room for calendar entries, special events, and a list of who's driving whom to the ball diamond. A back door painted with chalkboard paint provides space for favorite sayings, a recipe you want to try, or sketches by kids. The chalkboard over the counter keeps tabs on the grocery list. Just make sure you stock up on chalk.

• Prevent the ghost effect of the first words you write on a newly painted chalkboard by prepping it before you start writing. To prep, use the side of a chalk stick to completely cover the board with chalk; wipe down the board with a soft rag.

## THE TECHNIQUES:

For more about chalkboard paint, see "Special Paints" on page 185.

## THE PALETTE:

Sources, page 186

**CHALKBOARD PAINT**

**REGINA MIST**

**BAYBERRY**

**PORCELAIN**

*Garden Pizza*

Lay out 2 packages Crescent
Rolls on 15½ x 10½-inch
cookie sheet. Bake according
to package directions; cool.
— Cheese layer —
8 oz. cream cheese
½ c. salad dressing
1 t. onion flakes
½ t. each garlic, salt
Blend and spread on cooled crust.
— toppings —
1 c. chopped green pepper
1 c. chopped onion
1 c. chopped tomatoes
1 c. chopped black olives

Sprinkle on top and refrigerate
for several hours
before serving.

Cantaloupe
- Strawberries -
Flour

Borgia
Cappuccino
Café Late

*Above:*
The design of this
kitchen, including the
door and wall painted
with chalkboard paint,
mimics coffeehouse decor.

Opposite bottom:
Jars with screw lids
attached to the underside
of a shelf store
ingredients.

Left:
Chalkboard paint wraps
the center of the kitchen
with a swath of color
and messages.

Paint specially
formulated for use on
ceramic tiles
transforms 8×8-inch
tile squares into a
4-inch checkerboard.

MILK

## THE QUESTION:

*I loved white ceramic tile when I remodeled several years ago. Now I'd like more color in my kitchen. How can I paint installed ceramic tile?*

Below:
For a painterly effect, apply the paint with a brush and let the strokes show.

Bottom:
Fabrics and ribbons can inspire details such as the star and dots hand-painted using a small brush.

## THE ANSWER:

Installed or ready to install, ceramic tile is certainly paintable. A variety of paint products can do the job. Read the paint labels to decide which product is best for your situation.

## THE LESSONS:

• Soften a bold color scheme of red and white with a whisper-soft shade of blue on the walls. That surprising background works perfectly as a foil for the graphic hand-painted ceramic tiles. A bold color would detract from the fun.

• To paint ceramic tile, select a paint that works for your situation and carefully follow the manufacturer's instructions. If you skip a step, the results can't be guaranteed. This tile was painted using 2-ounce bottles of crafts paint that are suitable for painting tile. (Note: Check the label before painting. Some paints are not recommended for use with food. It's OK to use them for the backsplash tiles but not for tiles installed on the counter.)

• Integrate the bold red-and-white pattern into the scheme by repeating it on window treatments and accessories.

## THE TECHNIQUES:

For more about painting ceramic tile, see Chapter 4, "Walls," page 48.

## THE PALETTE:

Sources, page 186

**CALICO RED**          **SKY HIGH**

*A new kitchen in a vintage home needs to bridge generations. A painted finish makes it easy to build new cabinetry and give it an old-world look.*

# Visible character

## THE QUESTION:

*We would love to paint the stained cabinets in our traditional kitchen. Friends tell us that painted cabinets are too hard to maintain. Are we making a mistake?*

## THE ANSWER:

Painted cabinets, once harder to maintain than stained cabinets, now feature new tough finishes that stand up to wear in this busy area of the house. In addition, techniques such as distressing the finish to look worn mean that any additional wear blends in.

## THE LESSONS:

• Primary colors, such as red and yellow, provide a scheme with a lot of light and visual bounce. To make them work in a vintage house, shade the hues with black or gray to create a more subdued but still bright palette. Add accents of black or gray/stainless steel on appliances or accessories to make the red and yellow stand out.

• Paint in a kitchen can cover much more than floors and walls. In fact, with the popularity of wood floors and ceramic-tile walls, those surfaces might never see paint. But the cabinets? When you want to bring color into a kitchen, cabinetry offers the perfect canvas for a palette of two or more colors. It's easy if you paint base cabinets one color and the upper cabinets a second color, or paint an island to stand out and the rest of the cabinets to blend in.

• Experiment with a paint finish that yields the look of a fine antique. These cabinets were stained a dark maple and then painted red. (This is an option over previously stained cabinets. Make sure you prepare the surface by sanding the finish to accept a coat of paint.) The island cabinetry was left red, creating an unfitted look in keeping with the style of the early 1900s. The rest of the cabinets were given a coat of yellow paint over the red. Sanding along the edges reveals both the red and the stain, as if worn by age.

• Consider other surfaces for an aged painted treatment. The tin ceiling was painted a light yellow, then brushed with a tobacco-color glaze. The process brings out the pattern of the tin panels and helps the ceiling blend with the aged cabinetry.

## THE TECHNIQUES:

For more about preparing and painting wood cabinets, see "Surfaces and how to paint them," beginning on page 178.

The trick to an old finish is to brush on layers—dark maple stain, red paint, and yellow paint—then remove the layers in places to give the look of wear. Wood stained dark maple provides contrast in the back of some of the open cabinets.

This page:
Signs of wear give the
paint finish an aged
look on the upper and
lower cabinets. A layer
of red peeks through
the yellow paint and
complements the
red island.

## THE PALETTE:

Sources, page 187

**BARN RED + SALEM RED**    **MUSTARD**

The soaking tub nestles into an alcove under a white beaded ceiling outlined in a wallcovering painted ocean blue.

Embossed wallpaper combines Victorian appeal and modern color in one pretty package.

A freestanding cabinet painted to match the walls provides storage that's pretty and functional.

Install robe hooks to keep towels handy.

# Some things blue

## THE QUESTION:

*We're building a new master bathroom that's modern and nostalgic at the same time with a fabulous tub as the centerpiece. What can we do on the walls?*

## THE ANSWER:

For a look that fits both moods, hang embossed wallpaper on the walls and cover it with a surprising shade of blue.

## THE LESSONS:

• Primary colors used in pairs, such as blue and yellow, brighten a space. Combine them with white-painted woodwork and ceiling for a color scheme that's crisp. The trick is to combine several shades of blue and yellow to add interest to the palette.

• For a textured wall that features paint, start with an embossed wallpaper that requires paint for the finish coat. These wallcoverings, still popular in England, hide imperfections on old walls and add texture to new walls. To give a painted wallcovering added oomph in a room, provide visual relief with a wainscot or ceiling of white-painted beaded board.

• Embossed wallpaper provides the basis for mixing and matching other patterns, such as an allover floral fabric and a bold striped rug.

## THE TECHNIQUES:

For more about painting unfinished wood paneling, see "Surfaces and how to paint them," beginning on page 178.

## THE PALETTE:

Sources, page 187

**GULF STREAM**

# Not from scratch

## THE QUESTION:

*Our second bathroom that's used for guests and kids is serviceable but dated. We would like to update it without changing fixtures or cabinets. Is paint enough?*

## THE ANSWER:

Don't think of paint as a minor change. Spread it over floors, countertops, and walls for a guaranteed dramatic difference.

## THE LESSONS:

• Choose a neutral color scheme for a bathroom that's split between guests and kids. A bath that's too juvenile becomes dated even faster than '80s decor. Touches of black punctuate this neutral scheme of taupe and cream and add just a touch of energy.

• Gather paints suited for surfaces you need to finish, such as laminate countertops, vinyl flooring, and walls. Each of these surfaces can be painted but they may require slightly different products. The real key to success is preparation of the surfaces so the paint stays put and wears well.

## THE TECHNIQUES:

For more about painting vinyl flooring and laminate countertops, see "Surfaces and how to paint them," beginning on page 178.

## THE PALETTE:

Sources, page 187

**DIVINE WHITE**

**RELAXED KHAKI**

**BLACK OF NIGHT**

▶ **Every surface in this bathroom—vinyl flooring, laminate countertop, plaster walls, and wood cabinets—received a coat of paint.**

*A sponged finish gives a half bath metallic shimmer.*

# Easy glamour

## THE QUESTION:

*I've noticed metallic paints in the stores recently. How can I use this product?*

## THE ANSWER:

The cautious approach is to use one of these metal-like finishes in a small space such as a half bath. They're also perfect for everything from mirror frames to light fixtures.

## THE LESSONS:

• Let a metal finish be the star of the room by combining it with neutrals and wood tones. Bring in color as accessories.

• To try a metal technique, start by creating a sample board. The process usually involves painting the wall a base color; then sponging, brushing, or ragging a metallic glaze over the top. The technique you use determines the amount of metallic finish you leave on the wall. This same process can be used on furniture and accessories. Look for these products packaged as small as a half-pint.

## THE TECHNIQUES:

For more about special wall finishes, see Chapter 4, "Walls," beginning on page 40.

## THE PALETTE:

Sources, page 187

**METALLIC LEAFING SILVER**

**GARDEN WALL**

# Go bold

*A bathroom for kids should be just plain fun but ours is just plain. What's a parent to do?*

## THE ANSWER:

Bring out the markers and sheets of paper and let your kids doodle and draw. They'll inspire a fresh new color scheme—and maybe a few patterns—for their bathroom.

## THE LESSONS:

• Add pizzazz to an all-white room by washing color liberally over the walls. If the walls are already covered in white satin or semigloss, you won't even have to paint first. Mix a bright hue 1:1 with glazing liquid to create a finish you can brush on and brush off to give this striated effect.

• Freehand painting lends a more whimsical effect than stenciled patterns. Practice first, then add dots to the walls and plaid to random floor tiles. Choose paints for the surface you want to coat. Some crafts paints might work for both surfaces.

## THE TECHNIQUES:

For more about painting ceramic tile, see page 40 in Chapter 4, "Walls."

## THE PALETTE:

Sources, page 187

**OCEAN VOYAGE**

**SUNFLOWER**

**BERRY**

**COBALT**

**GRASS GREEN**

*Paint adds color and pattern to the walls and floors in this kids' bathroom.*

Striped walls and repainted cabinetry update this once-dated bathroom.

# Classic update

## THE QUESTION:

*Our classic old bath needs an update to enhance its fine features. How can we give it a lift without destroying its character?*

## THE ANSWER:

With paint of course! Use paint to call attention to tile, fixtures, flooring, and built-ins. Pick a few shades of one color that are perfect for the era of the room.

## THE LESSONS:

• A color scheme of white plus one color is the easiest to create. Add interest by including several shades of the single color.

• Call attention to the best features of the bathroom using paint. The wonderful white subway tile looks fresh again thanks to a paint treatment that pulls the color of the tile right up the walls. The stripe pattern features two shades of green with a fine white stripe.

• Update built-ins with a soft shade of any color. For even more vintage appeal, replace the knobs with glass ones and add a stencil to the drawer faces.

## THE TECHNIQUES:

For more about painting stripes, see "Do the Math," on page 185.

## THE PALETTE:

Sources, page 187

**HEMLOCK BUD**

**SPRING HILL**

# Suite style

## THE QUESTION:

I found a wallpaper I love for our master bathroom. How do I coordinate paint and wallpaper?

## THE ANSWER:

Paint doesn't always have to be the star of a room. It plays well in a supporting role too. Here's how to put it to work.

## THE LESSONS:

• Wallpaper and fabric provide perfect starting points for creating a color scheme. In fact, it's almost a foolproof way to ensure you'll love the colors in your room. The red-orange stripe of the wallcovering pops up again on the tub and the exterior of the French door. The secret is to use the stronger shade for just a little coverage.

• Use paint as a background, in this case on wainscot and molding painted a crisp white. Look for a paint product that's self-leveling when you paint woodwork. Brush on a coat and wait. The paint will level out as it dries. Any fine lines can be sanded away.

• Accent with paint. A graceful claw-foot tub looks even more inviting painted a warm shade of red. It's an appropriate color for a piece that's the focal point of the room. The exterior side of the door features red as well. It provides a surprising accent when the door is open and offers a hint of color when the door is closed.

• Add a little black to ground a color scheme. If you can't find the perfect piece of furniture in black, paint the piece you find. For a washable matte finish, consider using milk paint.

## THE TECHNIQUES:

For more about painting a variety of surfaces, see "Surfaces and how to paint them," beginning on page 178.

## THE PALETTE:

Sources, page 187

**BRAVADO RED**

Above:
Semigloss latex paint covers the old tub. The feet were stripped and replated in chrome.

Opposite above and bottom:
Use a touch of black paint, here on a stand, to ground any color scheme.

Left:
Red-orange paint on the door picks up the color of the bathtub.

CHAPTER 6 *Floors*

Floors are the
Rodney Dangerfield
of the home: After all, they get
no respect. From muddy shoes
to wet boots to rampaging kids,
floors just lie there and take it.
No wonder they can get a little
tired looking. Here's help. New
floor enamels in alkyd and water-
base formulations pair with durable
primers for finishes that look good and last
long. So instead of making do with the
floors you have, think of those worn
surfaces as a canvas for your creativity.
Soon you'll be adding a bit of paint here,
there, and everywhere.

Brush on a new look:
- Wood with stencils, page 86
- Painted porch floor, page 88
- Sisal rug, page 90
- Vinyl floorcloth, page 92

Use stencils to
add personality
to wood floors.

# Oak flooring

## THE QUESTION:

I have oak flooring throughout the first floor of my house. I love it but it's not too exciting. I was thinking of adding a design to my entry area. Am I crazy?

## THE ANSWER:

Hardwood floors provide a beautiful background for stencil patterns. Start with just a few to see if you really like them. If you don't, sand away the paint and apply polyurethane. If you're ready for more, here's how to get started.

## THE TECHNIQUES:

• Make sure the floor is protected with at least three coats of polyurethane, whether it is stained or painted.

• Wash the floor with a nonsoapy cleaner; let dry.

• Decide on the design and where you want it based on the room's dimensions. Draw the room to scale on graph paper. Use colored pencils to try out the stencil design on the graph paper plan. Once you like the look, lay out the location of the border on the flooring using a right angle, straightedge, and colored pencil. Apply painter's tape along the penciled lines; burnish the edges to seal the tape to the wood. Lightly sand areas. For the stenciled parts of the design, apply stencil adhesive to temporarily adhere the stencil to the floor.

• Try the painting technique on a scrap of finished flooring or in a hidden spot such as inside a closet. For the most control, use stencil cream and a large stencil brush (photo A). Brush away from the edges of the tape or stencil to keep paint from seeping underneath (photo B). Stencil cream takes a little while to dry, so be careful when moving the stencil from one spot to another.

• For interesting effects, use two or more colors of stencil cream. This technique lets you create shadows on patterns.

• Protect the finished design with two or more coats of clear polyurethane to match the rest of the wood flooring.

## THE PALETTE:

Sources, page 187

BLACK CHERRY          PALE YELLOW

# Porch floor

## THE QUESTION:

I'd like to try something fun and unexpected on the floor of our back porch. Any ideas?

## THE ANSWER:

Painted stripes give a fun look, but add this surprising twist: a top layer of chicken wire. Faux, of course.

## THE TECHNIQUES:

• Prepare the surface by scraping any loose paint, sanding, wiping with a tack cloth, and priming. Preparation is key to a finish that lasts. Paint with a durable floor enamel using a medium tone. Always read the paint label to make sure the product you're using is recommended for outdoor applications. For durability, apply a second coat; let dry.

• Tape off stripes in the direction of the wood flooring, using the dimension of the wood to determine the width of the stripes. Stripes can be as narrow as one board or as wide as a combination of several boards. This floor features a stripe pattern that's as close to 12 inches as possible. Burnish the edges of the tape to keep paint from bleeding underneath.

• Paint the darker stripes using a 4-inch roller and cloth roller cover (photo A). Recoat if necessary. Remove tape; let dry overnight.

• Stencil using a chicken-wire stencil, paint cream in white, and a medium-size stencil brush. Start in a corner and work across a section, moving the stencil and painting a new area once the paint dries (photo B). Be sure to mark the stencil registration marks on the floor as you work to ensure the pattern matches from section to section.

• Protect the finished floor with polyurethane suitable for exterior applications.

## THE PALETTE:

Sources, page 187

**GREAT GREEN**    **LEAP FROG**

*Above:*
*Use high-quality exterior paints for durability on porch floors.*

For a washable
finish on sisal rugs,
use semigloss paint.

How To Paint Just About Anything

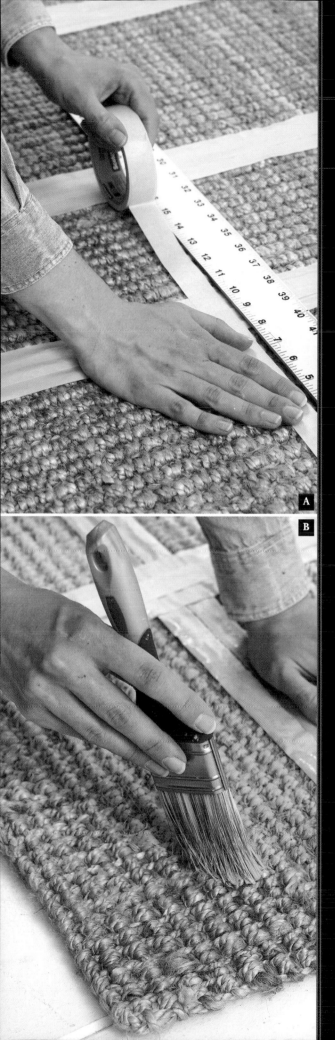

# Sisal rug

## THE QUESTION:

*Can I paint a sisal rug to go with my decor?*

## THE ANSWER:

Tightly woven sisal is easy to paint. For coarser sisal, plan a simple pattern and you'll be happy with the look.

## THE TECHNIQUES:

• To create this color-blocked treatment, use painter's tape to make sections 6 to 13 inches wide with 2 inches of the rug covered with tape between sections. Use a straightedge and the weave of the rug to guide the lines. Tape lengthwise stripes in the same manner but divide the rug into thirds, with 2 to 3 inches covered between each of the three stripes (photo A).

• Stencil each square with interior latex semigloss paint. Dip an old, flat trimming brush ¼ inch into the paint; pounce the brush vertically to cover each section (photo B). Apply paint colors in a random manner, one color per block. Remove tape; let dry.

• If you're painting a rug to match a room, use leftover paints from other projects in the room.

## THE PALETTE:

Sources, page 187

PEAS IN A POD

FRESH PEACHES

CANDY COATED

OCEAN DREAM

BICYCLE YELLOW

# Vinyl floor

## THE QUESTION:

I've heard you can use the back of vinyl flooring as a floorcloth. How do you paint it?

## THE ANSWER:

Vinyl flooring makes a great cut-and-paint project, but the same painting techniques work if your vinyl floor is installed.

## THE TECHNIQUES:

• Purchase a remnant of vinyl flooring and cut it to the size you want using a crafts knife. Let the geometric embossing in the vinyl influence the size and shape of the rug, or reverse the rug to the smooth back side.

• Thoroughly wash the vinyl flooring with detergent; let dry.

• Prime with a high-quality primer. If you don't know where to start, ask the experts at your local paint store to recommend a primer. Keep notes on how the primer works to make it easy to pick products for future projects.

• Base-coat the entire area with paint that coordinates with the primer. If you used an alkyd primer, use an alkyd top coat. If the primer is water-based, the top coat should be too.

• Tape off the inner area of the rug with painter's tape. Dip brushes into three colors and randomly apply the paint to the flooring, slightly blending the colors. (This project uses three pastel semigloss hues.) Use a special paint pad to blend the wet, streaked paint (photo A). Repeat the process until the desired look is achieved. Remove tape; let dry.

• Hand-paint the border squares by following the embossed design. Or, use a T-square and straightedge to mark blocks. Apply paint using a 2-inch trim brush; let dry.

• Use a foam roller to coat the leaf stamp; use as little paint as necessary and practice the technique on a sample board. Carefully press the stamp on the painted surface; lift the stamp straight up to keep from smudging the design (photo B).

• Protect the finished floorcloth with two or three coats of clear polyurethane.

## THE PALETTE:

Sources, page 187

**FAIRWAY MIST**

**PALE DAFFODIL**

**FOUNTAIN SPOUT**

**SHIRE GREEN**

Freshen worn vinyl flooring with any water-base floor paint or use regular paint and protect the finish with polyurethane.

Use remnants of vinyl flooring and paint the back to make floorcloths.

# Bedrooms

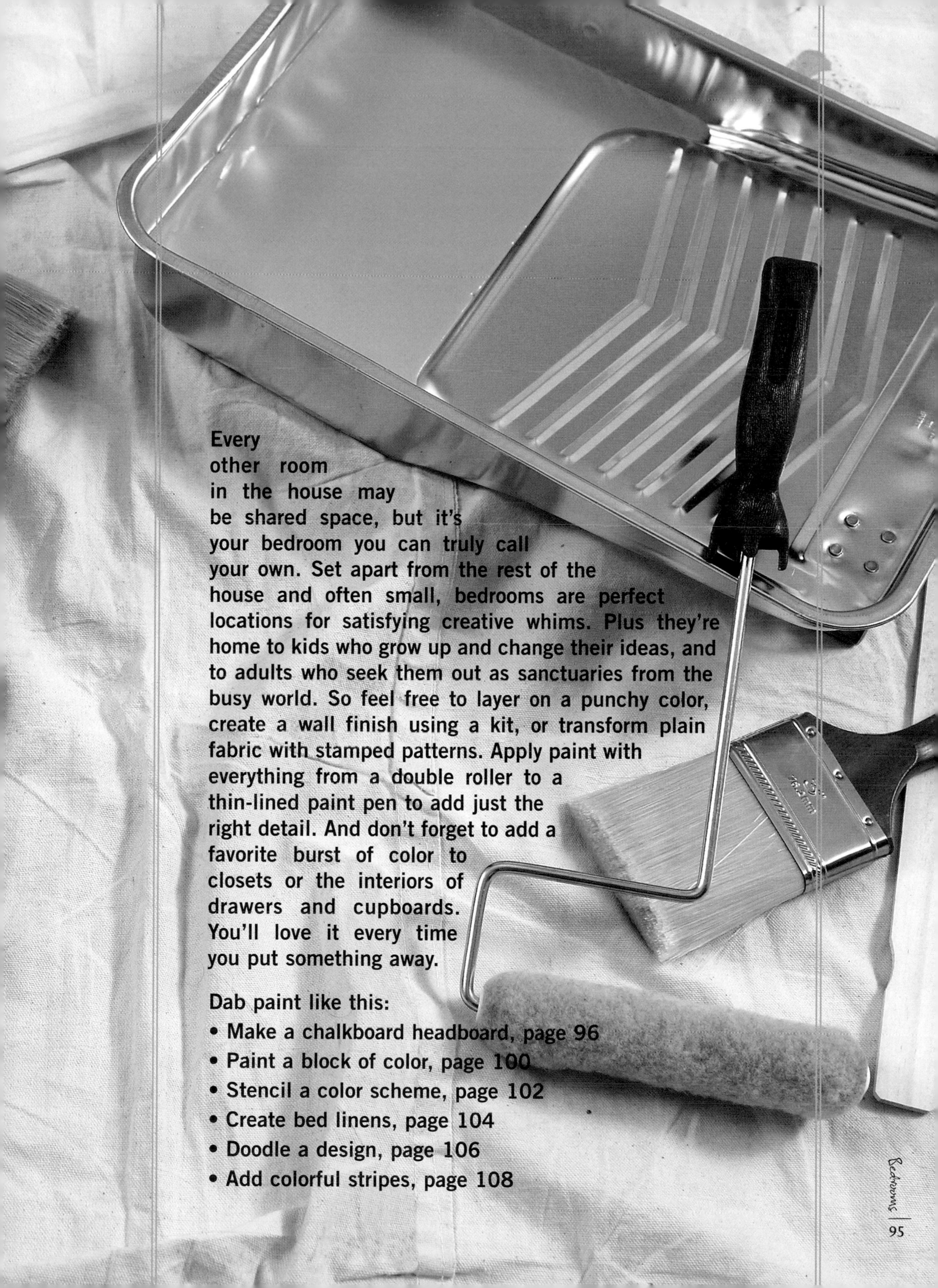

Every
other room
in the house may
be shared space, but it's
your bedroom you can truly call
your own. Set apart from the rest of the
house and often small, bedrooms are perfect
locations for satisfying creative whims. Plus they're
home to kids who grow up and change their ideas, and
to adults who seek them out as sanctuaries from the
busy world. So feel free to layer on a punchy color,
create a wall finish using a kit, or transform plain
fabric with stamped patterns. Apply paint with
everything from a double roller to a
thin-lined paint pen to add just the
right detail. And don't forget to add a
favorite burst of color to
closets or the interiors of
drawers and cupboards.
You'll love it every time
you put something away.

Dab paint like this:
• Make a chalkboard headboard, page 96
• Paint a block of color, page 100
• Stencil a color scheme, page 102
• Create bed linens, page 104
• Doodle a design, page 106
• Add colorful stripes, page 108

Fabric walls recede into the background when a painted headboard takes center stage in this sophisticated bedroom.

How To Paint Just About Anything

# Take note

## THE QUESTION:

*My all-neutral bedroom needs a surprising twist. I've added a colorful quilt, but it isn't enough. I don't really want to add any more color. What can I do?*

## THE ANSWER:

Sometimes you can create the best decorating surprise by using a common material in a fresh way. Why not bring a slate-color chalkboard into the bedroom? This headboard might appear hefty, but it's made from thin plywood coated with chalkboard paint and edged with picture molding.

## THE LESSONS:

• Neutrals offer serenity in bedrooms, but it's important to make sure a neutral bedroom isn't just boring. The trick is to bring in color slowly, adding just enough to add interest without jarring the peace of the place. Adding strong colors in accents, such as bedding, ensures you easily can change the look in a snap.

• Surprises can come in neutrals too. That's the case with this dramatic headboard in black and silver. The soft black is really chalkboard paint rolled over thin plywood. It's an unexpected finish for a sophisticated bedroom. A metallic paint with real silver covers up plastic molding in just one coat. The silver will age and tarnish over time.

• Vintage pieces of furniture can look young and fresh with a fun paint treatment (see page 99). If you don't want to stray too far from the vintage appeal, try a paint finish that looks old. Metallic spray paints in silver offer a quick way to update brassy hardware. Layers of milk paint in tones from warm yellow to steely gray layer over the formerly stained finish. To get this effect, apply primer to the surface using a brush and irregular strokes. Add color to edges and drawer fronts, applying the various colors in a random manner; top-coat with gray. To allow the colors to show through, lightly sand the surface or use a plastic scrubber to remove some of the paint. Protect the finish from wear with two light coats of matte polyurethane.

## THE TECHNIQUES

For more about chalkboard paint, see "Special Paints" on page 185.

Plastic molding forms a frame around a sheet of plywood finished with chalkboard paint. Keep the chalk handy.

Affordable and plentiful at used-furniture shops, a dresser like this looks young again thanks to an easy paint finish.

Use semigloss paint to update the frame of a vintage chair before adding new fabric to the seat and back.

Create your own art or leave a note on this oversize message board.

## THE PALETTE:

Sources, page 187

**CHALKBOARD BLACK**

**POLAR BEAR**

**ANTIQUE FRESCO**

**CLOUD COVER**

**CHILLY MORNING**

**METALLIC LEAFING SILVER**

# Block party

## THE QUESTION:

*Guests are due to arrive for a visit in a few weeks. My guest room is boring white, but I can't afford to do anything but paint. Is there any way to make it a more welcoming room?*

## THE ANSWER:

Squeeze life into a dull room with a liberal dose of bold color, but don't do the expected and paint the entire wall. Instead create color blocks that march around the room.

## THE LESSONS

• Build on the white paint already in place in a room. This simple treatment layers on top of white walls and uses the white space as a visual rest from bold color. Select two or three shades of color adjacent or one color away on the paint chip card. A color scheme of white plus one color is simple to create if you use several shades for interest.

• Be flexible with painted blocks. It's not possible in most rooms to create blocks all in the same size, so vary their widths for added interest and less math work. The room's dimensions will determine the size of the blocks. Measure the width of each wall, divide it into equal parts, and allow space between blocks and in the corners. Try to keep each window and door within one color area.

• Use painter's tape to create your pattern and a spirit level to mark the blocks on the wall. Tape off the blocks and burnish the tape edges to keep paint from seeping under. Roll on the paint.

• Create art for the room by using the leftover paint to cover several squares of artist's canvas. Hang the artwork within the walls' color blocks.

## THE TECHNIQUES:

For more about painting patterned walls, see "Do the Math," on page 185.

## THE PALETTE:

Sources, page 187

**GLORIOUS GOLD**    **LEMON SORBET**

*Opposite:*
*White walls provide the perfect backdrop for this colorful paint treatment that maintains the white paint as horizontal and vertical edging.*

*Above:*
*Vary the shades of the color blocks for added interest. Add furniture and accessories to contrast with the colorful walls.*

# Swedish by design

*Opposite:*
Serenity prevails in this master bedroom thanks to a one-color scheme of soft yellow. Every surface, including furniture and trim, is painted the same hue.

*Above:*
Cool blue pairs with warm yellow in the master bathroom. The hand-painted vine and flowers include shades of blue and yellow for consistency.

## THE QUESTION:

*I really love light, almost neutral shades, and I plan to use them in my master bedroom and bathroom. How can I keep the spaces serene without making them boring?*

## THE ANSWER:

The choice of color and sheen is crucial. Opt for a color such as this sunny pale yellow that changes with the light throughout the day. That way one color actually becomes many. If you select the same color of paint in a variety of sheens, you can also vary the perceived hue.

## THE LESSONS:

• Consider buying paint from one of the boutique paint companies that offer colors composed of many pigments. Several brands of paint on the market include as many as seven pigments in one can of paint. These complex paint formulas are friends to light and become luminous in sunlight or lamplight.

• For added luminosity, juxtapose warm and cool colors, such as the yellow in the bedroom with the blue-green in the bathroom and the greens and yellows of the vines and flowers painted over the bed and in the bathroom.

• Vary the sheen of paint for added interest. You might choose a matte finish for the walls, a satin finish for a dresser or side table, and a gloss sheen for a lamp base. Each sheen absorbs and reflects light differently.

• Decide on a focal point wall and add a painted design for even more interest. A vine topping the windows above the headboard reflects the owners' Swedish heritage. Although this pattern was hand-painted by an artist, you can find similar stencil patterns by doing an online search for Scandinavian stencil borders.

## THE TECHNIQUES:

For more about painting a variety of surfaces, see "Surfaces and how to paint them," beginning on page 178.

## THE PALETTE:

Sources, page 187

EGGNOG          MEADOW LIGHT

# Strokes of pattern

### THE QUESTION:

*I want my bedroom walls white and the color in my bedding. I'd love to create my own bedding designs using the colors I love. Can I really paint fabric? Will it stand up to laundering?*

### THE ANSWER:

Several companies offer products for painting fabrics. If you follow their directions, you'll be able to launder the finished products and love the look for years.

### THE LESSONS:

• Paint offers the perfect material for creating the one-of-a-kind bedding or fabric you just can't find or afford in the marketplace. New paint products offer a variety of techniques and finishes. Stencil creams allow the most control of the paint. Textile mediums mix with any water-base paint and make it usable on fabrics. In most cases, ironing sets the paint.

• Designs can be applied using freehand brushstrokes or created using stencils. It's best to create a free-form design if you plan to use brushstrokes. Sponge rollers work great over a stencil. The key is to apply paint in very thin coats. If you apply paint thickly, it may seep beyond the design.

• Not every fabric accepts paint, so it's crucial to try some samples first. Begin by washing and drying the fabric; do not use detergent or softener because they may affect the way the paint adheres to the fabric. Smooth fabric woven from natural fibers, such as linen and cotton, works best. Make sure you back up the fabric you're painting with a sheet of plastic until the paint dries. Some paint may seep through the fabric.

### THE TECHNIQUES:

For more about painting fabric, see "Surfaces and how to paint them," beginning on page 178.

For more about painting fabric, see "Surfaces and how to paint them," beginning on page 178.

### THE PALETTE:

Sources, page 187

**BAYOU**    **PINK PUNCH**    **SHALLOW SEA**

*Above:*
Freehand designs give these ready-made linens a designer look. Use painter's tape, stencils, and freehand patterns, alone or in combination, to create a suite of bedding linens.

Painted linens add color and personality to this cottage bedroom. Coordinated painted pieces should be laundered with the same frequency so they age consistently.

# Home graffiti

## THE QUESTION:

*I saw a magazine photo of a cabinet covered with line drawings created with paint pens. I love it! Can I really do this on the walls and furniture in my bedroom?*

## THE ANSWER:

This technique using paint pens or permanent markers might be the perfect way to release your inner artist, and it is reversible. If you change your mind, recoat the walls with a stain-blocking primer and you'll be right back where you started—with a blank canvas.

## THE LESSONS:

• Start with a minimal color palette, such as a black paint pen or permanent marker on walls painted a midtone color, such as yellow, pink, or blue. You could also use a hot shade of orange, lime green, or pink, and a white paint pen.

• Find your inspiration for patterns in books of architectural drawings, historical fabrics, illustrations of stage sets, and wallpapers. Take these inspirations and make them bigger than life for this fun effect. Molding painted around the ceiling creates the look of a three-dimensional border without the cost. Embellishments with paint pens turn a simple mirror into an elegant accent. More doodles create candelabras over the "fireplace" mantel.

• Start by creating patterns on big sheets of foam-core board or poster board. Hold these up to the wall to make sure you like them; make changes before you tackle the walls. When you're satisfied, sketch the design in pencil on the walls with as few lines as possible, putting more details on the elements you want to highlight. Stay loose and let your lines wiggle to lend humor and freshness.

## THE TECHNIQUES:

For more about primers, see "To Prime or Not?" on page 175.

## THE PALETTE:

Sources, page 187

**FROSTED LEMON**

*Above:*
Doodles made using a paint pen or permanent marker transform a plain bedroom.

*Opposite and left:*
Almost any surface works for this fun technique. Try it on furniture, lampshades, walls, and fabric.

# Growing room

## THE QUESTION:

How can you turn a boring box of a bedroom into a space that suits an 8-year-old boy now, yet still works when he turns 16?

## THE ANSWER:

Eliminate age-specific decorating options such as cartoon characters and fire truck wallpaper. Opt instead for the universal appeal of rugby stripes and a palette of shaded primary colors plus green applied in solid swaths.

## THE LESSONS:

• For a boy-friendly space, think well-washed rugby shirts and faded denim jeans for a muted palette that's sure to complement your son's stuff. Paint the walls a faded green hue; add traditional rugby colors, such as shaded tones of red, blue, and yellow.

• Paint stripes just above the baseboard to visually raise the height of a standard 8-foot-tall room. Vary the width of the stripes from wide to narrow. Then wrap the stripes around the room, letting them duck behind furniture, to give the room a sense of energy and fun. To make the stripes, use a level to find the horizontal line; pencil it in. Look for painter's tape in a range of widths from ½ inch to 3 inches and use multiples of these widths to mask off the stripes.

• Pick paints to suit the projects: scrubbable paint for the walls, spray metallic paint to cover a vintage filing cabinet turned dresser, and paint thinned with glazing liquid to add a colorful wash to an unfinished wood chest.

## THE TECHNIQUES:

For more about painting stripes, see "Do the Math" on page 185.

## THE PALETTE:

Sources, page 187

**SCENERY HILL**

**BRICKLE**

**CHILI**

**SAMBUCCA**

An old metal filing cabinet looks hip again thanks to a coat of spray paint.

Borders wrap around the baseboard in this fun boy's room. Use varying sizes of painter's tape to create the stripes.

Pick the color scheme for a
boy's bedroom from a
favorite rugby shirt. Use a
favorite washed shade for
the walls and add stripes of
the boldest hues.

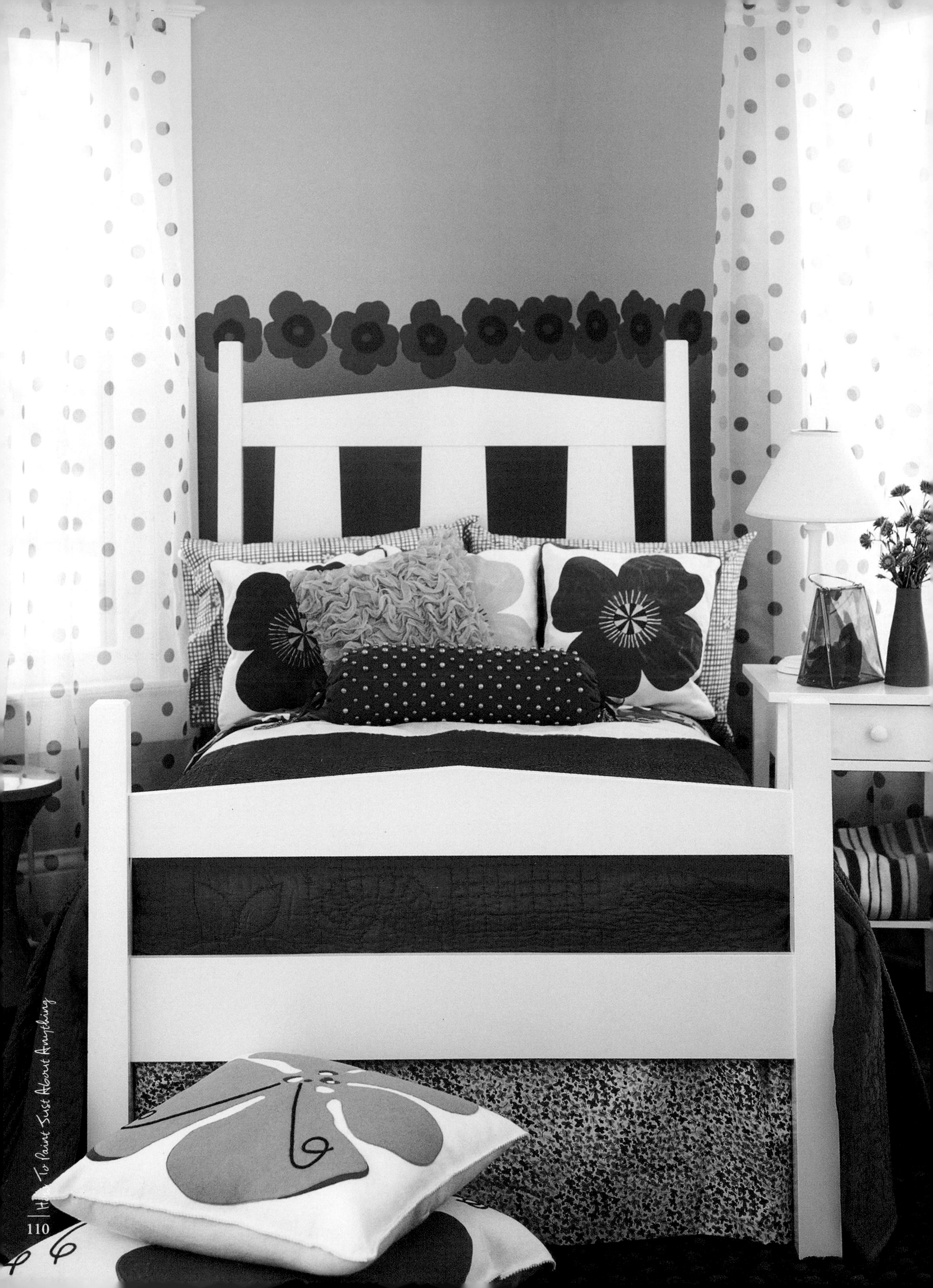

Opposite: *Create the look of wainscot by painting two shades of color on the walls and adding a fanciful flower stencil as a border between colors.*

Top and above: *Flowers on ready-made pillows inspired the flower stencil used on the wall. A single stencil, rotated along the walls, adds a fun touch.*

# Flower power

## THE QUESTION:

*We just painted a bedroom bright pink, but it's just too pink. I feel like I'm in a bubble gum factory. Can I salvage this hue?*

## THE ANSWER:

It's great you're trying new hues, but the secret to using strong color is balance. You're sure to love the room if you bring in other strong colors, such as tangerine and deep violet, and play them against crisp white.

## THE LESSONS:

• If your house is filled with neutrals and shaded colors, try bright hues in rooms with doors, such as bedrooms. That's a great way to stretch your decorating palette.

• Gather the bold colors all together on the walls by painting the top 40 percent of the walls the lighter shade of pink and the bottom 60 percent the deeper shade of fuchsia. Introduce the tangerine and deep violet as a flower wainscot that's stenciled over the edge between hues. This stencil makes use of a single flower that's randomly placed as a border.

• Edge brights with white for a look everyone can live with. That means painting furniture and woodwork white for visual breathing space.

## THE TECHNIQUES:

For more about stenciling, see page 183.

## THE PALETTE:

Sources, page 187

LOVABLE                    INVIGORATE

AMARYLLIS

# CHAPTER 8

# Furniture

There's universal appeal in taking something you like and turning it into something you love. That's why paint is such a miracle worker when it comes to furniture. It covers worn surfaces, gives a ho-hum piece a style makeover, and adds a touch of whimsy to the most serious pieces. So whether your furniture came from Mom and Dad, the cheapest discount store, the curb on trash day, or the "as is" section of the furniture store, here's how to stamp it with your personal style using paint.

Try these paint redos:
• Add a monogram to a plastic tabletop, page 115
• Stripe a laminate dresser, page 117
• Make wood look like fabric, page 120
• Paint a glass tabletop, page 122

# Wood cabinet

*Are there some tips I can use for painting any piece of wood furniture?*

## THE ANSWER:

The best advice is to carefully read the labels on paint products. Most labels include recommendations for specific preparation and painting techniques.

## THE TECHNIQUES:

• Preparation is the key to laying a foundation for a professional-looking paint finish. Paint doesn't cover up flaws. It makes them look worse. Start the preparation process by scrubbing the surface with TSP to remove dirt and sanding to remove any loose paint and to even out irregular areas. Fill holes with a wood filler, sand, and remove dust using a tack cloth. Prime the surface; let dry. If you're using a dark-tone paint for the top coat, have the primer tinted to match.

• Apply the base coat. A paint roller may leave a slightly textured finish, and a brush can leave marks unless you brush as little as possible and use a light touch. If the paint you're using is self-leveling, roll on the paint and brush over it while it's still wet. Most of the brush marks will disappear as the paint dries. Add any decorative paint techniques. This cabinet features an irregular brush of white paint to accent the front panels and drawers. If you add a paint finish, top off the entire piece with two coats of clear polyurethane in a matte finish. Let the finish dry thoroughly between coats.

## THE PALETTE:

Sources, page 187

**WILD DAISY**

# Nesting tables

## THE QUESTION:

*I found a set of nesting tables with plastic inserts. Can I paint plastic?*

## THE ANSWER:

Manufacturers have developed spray paints for plastic but many of the crafts paints will work, too. Just check the label.

## THE TECHNIQUES:

• Follow the directions opposite to prepare and paint the tables. Use black milk paint to accentuate the simple lines of the table.

• Paint the tops of two of the tables with crafts paint in lime. Crafts paints, available in a huge selection of colors, are perfect when you're painting only a little bit.

• Use a letter stencil to create a monogram for one of the plastic table inserts. To do this project, trace the letters onto a piece of adhesive shelf paper. (Remember that the sticky side of the shelf paper should face the underside of the plastic tabletop insert.) Cut out the letters leaving narrow strips in a few places to keep the letters connected. Remove the backing and stick the monogram to the underside of the insert. Use painter's tape and plastic sheeting to protect the table from overspray; spray-paint the underside of the plastic tabletop with white paint. Remove adhesive paper. If any glue residue remains, clean it using rubbing alcohol.

## THE PALETTE:

Sources, page 187

**PITCH BLACK**

**FROSTED WHITE**

**YELLOW CITRON**

# Wicker chair

## THE QUESTION:

*Can I paint wicker so it's something other than natural finish or white?*

## THE ANSWER:

Wicker takes to spray paint, but it's tricky to cover every bit of it using a brush. To give wicker a modern look, paint it with a matte-finish paint.

## THE TECHNIQUES:

• Prepare the wicker chair for painting by sanding it lightly if the surface is shiny and washing it with TSP; let dry for 24 hours.

• If you don't have access to a paint sprayer, consider renting one for this paint job. Prime the chair using a primer tinted to match the top coat. Frequently change directions when spraying to ensure even coverage. Let primer dry twice as long as the directions require.

• Apply a top coat of matte paint to give the chair modern appeal. If you're concerned about stains, especially on the arms, top areas with a light coat of matte polyurethane.

## THE PALETTE:

Sources, page 187

**GALVESTON GRAY**

# Laminate dresser top

## THE QUESTION:

How can I give discount furniture a designer look?

## THE ANSWER:

Add color and pattern using a simple taping technique and primer made especially for use on laminate.

## THE TECHNIQUES:

• Practice restraint when painting a simple dresser with a modern attitude. In this case a painted finish was added only to the top.

• To prepare laminate for painting, sand lightly; remove dust using a tack cloth.

• Use painter's tape to lay out a pattern of stripes on the dresser top. Use a tape measure to establish the center of the pattern and to create a wide center stripe. To create a no-measure pattern for the diagonal stripes, apply tape so it just abuts the piece next to it until the entire top is covered. To create the pattern, remove every other piece of tape.

• Prime the surface using a primer made for laminate; let dry. Apply one or two coats of the finish color in semigloss paint; let dry. To remove the tape, use a straightedge and crafts knife to very lightly score along the tape edges. Carefully remove the tape.

## THE PALETTE:

Sources, page 187

**BUTTERSCOTCH**

# Cane headboard

## THE QUESTION:

*Do I have to use one paint for wood and another for the caning on my headboard?*

## THE ANSWER:

Most paints will cover both surfaces, but always test products in a hidden spot so you're sure they'll work. That's a basic rule to follow no matter what you're painting.

## THE TECHNIQUES:

• Prepare the wood surfaces for painting following the directions on page 114.

• To create stripes on the caning, apply painter's tape and burnish the edges to keep paint from seeping underneath. The stripe pattern is subtle due to a finish coat that's close in color to the natural tones of the caning.

• Paint wood and caning using a roller. Take care to blot the roller on newspaper before painting the stripes. If your roller is too full of paint, some might seep under the tape edges.

## THE PALETTE:

Sources, page 187

**GOLDEN DUNES**

# Plywood ottoman base

## THE QUESTION:

*Can I use metallic paint on wood?*

## THE ANSWER:

Why not? For a slightly industrial look, metallic paint adds the perfect finish. Most metallic paints are suitable for use on wood.

## THE TECHNIQUES:

• Shop home centers as well as paint and crafts stores for metallic paints that suit the look you want. For a glossy finish, apply a high-shine spray paint. For textured metal surfaces, use a hammered-metallic spray paint. For a metal finish that ages, select a paint finish that includes real metal that will tarnish.

• To prepare the plywood base of this rolling coffee table/ottoman for painting, sand the surface and remove dust with a tack cloth. Prime all sides as well as top and bottom to keep the plywood from warping.

• Spray or roll on the metal finish of your choice. Apply several thin coats of paint rather than one thick coat.

## THE PALETTE:

Sources, page 187

**METALLIC SILVER**

# Wood headboard

## THE QUESTION:

*I love cottage style. How can I paint a piece without copying the white look I see almost everywhere?*

## THE ANSWER:

Think beyond white paint to stencils that let you play with pattern and soft colors.

## THE TECHNIQUES:

• Prepare the surface for painting following the directions on page 114. To give a piece of furniture an aged painted finish, apply the base coat using a brush and varying the direction as you paint. This will add texture to the surface and provide a base for the stencil.

• Use a stencil made for an allover wall treatment to create the look of fabric. Spray the back of the stencil with stencil adhesive, center it in the middle of the headboard, and press it in place. For a variegated look, put dabs of blue, green, and gray on a paper plate. Roll a foam roller through the paint, roll it over newspaper to remove some of the paint, and then paint over the stencil. Remove the stencil and move it to another spot on the headboard after the paint has dried. Repeat this process until the entire headboard is stenciled.

• To protect the finish, apply two coats of matte or satin polyurethane, letting the finish dry between coats.

## THE PALETTE:

Sources, page 187

**APPLE GREEN**

**SOFT GREY**

**JAMAICAN SEA**

# Wood table base

## THE QUESTION:

*I found a wonderful old marble tabletop with a painted design in gold. What can I paint to go with it?*

## THE ANSWER:

Search for a base without a top to paint in metallic gold. Add dots along the edge for a folksy contrast to dressy marble.

## THE TECHNIQUES:

• Prepare an old piece of furniture for painting by following the instructions on page 114. Be especially careful to make sure the paint you're covering is intact.

• Be playful with paint. A serious piece of furniture, such as a marble top, might seem too formal for today's relaxed living. Dress it down with a whimsical paint treatment of dots applied using a paint pen.

• Paint pens are fabulous tools for applying all kinds of handwork to painted furniture. Because you use them like a pen, they allow the same control you have when writing. Look for paint pens with narrow tips for delicate work and fatter tips for bold strokes. Use them to write words, edge other painted designs, or add details such as dots and dashes.

## THE PALETTE:

Sources, page 187

### METAL LEAFING GOLD

### GLOSS BLACK

# Glass tabletop

## THE QUESTION:

*My new table came with a glass tabletop I want to paint. How do I do it?*

## THE ANSWER:

Painting the reverse side of glass gives it an interesting translucent effect. Search for paints suited for use on glass at a crafts store.

## THE TECHNIQUES:

• Factor in the green tint of glass when picking colors for any glass tabletop. If you're not sure what color to use, pick a hue and try it in a small area of the glass to see how it looks mixed with green. Always check the color by looking through the glass from the top side. Here, the color is backed with solid black to keep light from filtering through. Use a straightedge blade to remove your trial spot.

• To leave a clear glass border, trace the shape of the glass top on paper and make a border stencil composed of pieces. Use stencil adhesive to adhere the stencils in place.

• Apply all paints to the underside of the tabletop. Use a metallic paint pen to add a border and row of dots as accents along the painted edge; let dry. Remember that the first layer of paint will be the top layer when the glass top is reversed. Apply several light coats of spray paint, letting the paint dry between coats. If you want light to filter through the paint, seal the surface with two light coats of polyurethane. To keep light from filtering through the paint, coat the back with black paint; seal with two light coats of polyurethane. Let the finish cure (this may take a week or more, depending on the humidity levels) before setting the top on the base.

## THE PALETTE:

Sources, page 187

**TURNING LEAF**

**PALE GOLD**

**BLACK**

# CHAPTER 9

# Work & Play

Never underestimate the power of paint to set the mood. In hardworking spaces and rooms designed for fun, paint in all its many hues can be playful, energetic, serene, warm, relaxing, and more. That's why it makes the perfect decorating material when you want to transform a basic box of a room into a space with a mission. Pick bright colors such as orange and yellow to perk up the energy level in a laundry or kids' playroom; opt for watery blues, soft grays, and sage greens in an adult play space that's all about relaxing.

Solve problems with paint:
- Disguise bad walls, page 126
- Brush on stripes, page 130
- Transform unfinished furniture, page 134
- Brighten a laundry, page 136
- Paint concrete floors, page 138

# Dream studio

## THE QUESTION:

*What can I use to cover up all the imperfections on my studio's plaster walls?*

## THE ANSWER:

Old walls seem to be always on the move. Even after repairs, cracks reappear, traveling up and down the walls. The easiest way to cover up cracks and dents is by using matte paint with a textured finish. Look for products that promise the texture of stone or suede.

## THE LESSONS:

• Textured paints go up easily using a roller and disguise the cracks. Darker shades of these textured finishes hide imperfections best.

• Durable floor paints offer super simple finishes for worn floors as well. They multiply light, too, in a space where the walls are dark. To keep the floors looking good, use an alkyd floor enamel that's easy to wash. If you want a matte finish, coat the floor with two or more coats of flat polyurethane.

• For a country modern look, restrict the palette to neutrals and add interest with contrast. That's why white and charcoal make effective partners in this spare studio. Keeping the background colors neutral allows accent colors to follow the whims of fashion.

## THE TECHNIQUES:

For more about painting floors and walls, see "Surfaces and how to paint them," on page 178.

## THE PALETTE:

Sources, page 187

**RIVER SHALE**

A paint with a textured stone finish covers up problem walls.

CUSTOM HATCHING
2¢ an egg or 4¢ a Chix,
Turkeys 3¢ an egg or 5¢ a Chix
Ducks 3¢ an egg or 5¢ a Duckling
ALLEN KELLER

A rustic worktable made from galvanized pipe and slabs of wood offers plenty of work space in this studio.

How To Paint Just About Anything

**Below:**
*A combing tool pulled through the glaze diagonally gives the illusion of woven fabric rather than a painted pattern.*

**Opposite:**
*With its roots in fashion, the plaid paint treatment on the walls in this 6×7-foot kitchenette makes the best-dressed list.*

## THE QUESTION:
*Any ideas for giving a small space big style?*

## THE ANSWER:

Soft colors and small patterns can make a small space simply forgettable. But who won't remember a room finished in a bold plaid and stripe? This project will challenge your math and painting skills.

## THE LESSONS:

• Pick a strong but neutral palette for a complicated painting technique. After all, you want to love the look for a long time. Camel, cream, and black provide the base; red adds a shot of pizzazz.

• The technique involves painting a base coat of camel then taping off the stripes before painting the pattern. The paint, mixed two parts to one part glazing liquid, looks like fabric due to the effect created by diagonally pulling a combing tool through wet glaze.

## THE TECHNIQUES:

For more about painting cabinets and floors, see "Surfaces and how to paint them," on page 178.

## THE PALETTE:
Sources, page 187

**FAMILIAR BEIGE**

**DOMINO**

**TANAGER**

# Style down under

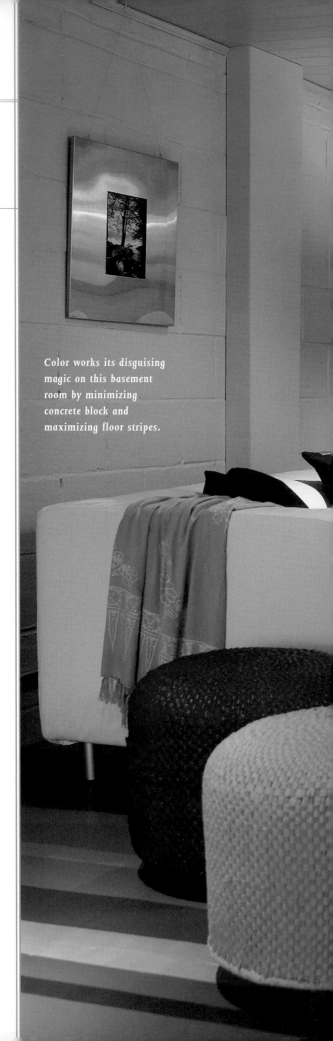

## THE QUESTION:

*We call our low-light basement family room "the dungeon." The dog won't even use it. What can we do to make it more inviting?*

## THE ANSWER:

Use the mood-raising qualities of color to make any basement space feel warmer, brighter, and more fun.

## THE LESSONS:

• Search for your color palette in favorite objects, fabrics, or books. A child's alligator cutout inspired the palette of this basement room. Ground the color scheme by combining all or most of the colors in one signature piece. That's the strategy behind painting stripes on the concrete floor.

• In an underground space, start with warm colors such as yellow-green and golden yellow. They'll make the room seem warmer and immediately make the space more inviting. Be sure to test paint colors in dark spaces. You may find you can use much brighter hues than you can in a sun-filled space. Colors here will be much less affected by changing light and reflections, but watch for the yellowing effects of lightbulbs.

• Use paint to cover up problems and create illusions. Paint minimizes the concrete-block walls, covers up a concrete floor, and refaces the brick fireplace. A bold green wall at one end of the space steps forward to minimize the room's length and works in tandem with the painted stripes that visually widen the long, narrow room.

• Spread color around with accents such as wicker ottomans painted red and green and a lampshade painted silver and embellished with dots.

## THE TECHNIQUES:

To learn more about painting concrete, wood paneling, wicker, and brick, see "Surfaces and how to paint them," beginning on page 178.

Color works its disguising magic on this basement room by minimizing concrete block and maximizing floor stripes.

A hollow-core door spray-painted with hammered aluminum paint pairs with a vintage stool freshened with silver and red paint.

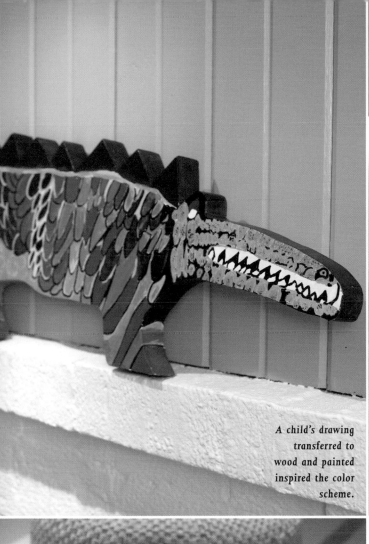

*A child's drawing transferred to wood and painted inspired the color scheme.*

*Use white upholstery to provide visual relief from color and pattern.*

*Paint a floor in wide stripes of light and dark gray before adding narrow stripes of brighter colors. Use painter's tape to create the pattern.*

## THE PALETTE:

Sources, page 187

**TURNING LEAF**

**CUSTOM COLOR**

**LIGHT GRAY**

**RED CURRANT**

**MEDIUM GRAY**

**SILVER HAMMERED**

# Home work

THE QUESTION:

*I need space to work at home, but in my small apartment I only have room in my dining room for a desk. How can I make a work area look like it belongs?*

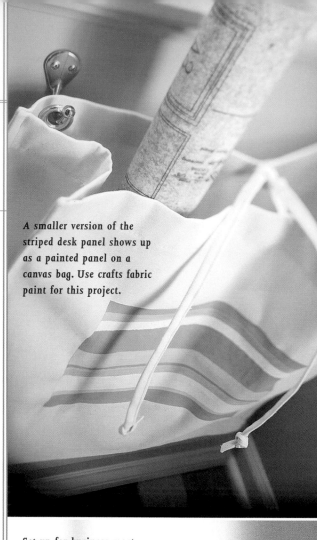

A smaller version of the striped desk panel shows up as a painted panel on a canvas bag. Use crafts fabric paint for this project.

## THE ANSWER:

Search for pieces of unfinished furniture that work together to create the look of a hutch you can use for work and for entertaining. Use paint to help the desk coordinate with your dining room.

## THE LESSONS:

• Unfinished furniture comes in a variety of serviceable pieces that might not be exactly your style. That's easy to remedy. To give generic unfinished furniture a fresh look, make some alterations. For this desk and hutch, the drawer handles were removed and replaced with double holes drilled through the drawer fronts. A ¼-inch plywood back added to the open hutch provides space to paint a chalkboard and striped memo board.

• For a personal space, spread paint on everything from the desk to the accessories. Chalkboard paint inside upper shelves and along the center back provides space for notes. Blocks of chalkboard paint on the fronts of buckets make erasable labels. Painted stripes on the back of the desk, repeated as labels on buckets and bags, continue the color scheme of blue-gray, orange, and yellow-green.

• Look to striped wallpaper and fabric for inspiration for the spacing of the painted stripes. Use varying widths of painter's tape to create the stripe patterns.

Set up for business most days, this desk/hutch can be changed into party central by stashing the office gear, setting out the appetizers, and writing the menu on the chalkboard paint.

## THE TECHNIQUES:

For more about painting new wood, see "Surfaces and how to paint them," beginning on page 178.

## THE PALETTE:

Sources, page 187

**LIME GRANITA**

**EXCITING ORANGE**

**NOTABLE HUE**

**HINTING BLUE**

LAUNDRY 15¢

Wide yellow stripes
painted over a base of
white give this laundry a
shot of sunshine even on
dreary days.

Wire baskets once used at a swimming pool provide portable storage for laundry supplies.

Shelves and hooks help organize laundry gear.

# Wash day

## THE QUESTION:

*I'll never love doing laundry, but I want to like my laundry room. What can I do to transform it?*

## THE ANSWER:

Start with your favorite color whether or not it's a color used in the rest of your house. If you have several favorites, pick the color that makes you feel energetic rather than soothed.

## THE LESSONS:

• Weekly chores deserve pleasant surroundings, so if your laundry area is stuck in a dingy basement or garage, it's time to get painting. Pick the paint type to suit the surfaces you're painting, from concrete to drywall to paneling. After all, you don't want a surface that requires a lot of work to maintain.

• Paint offers unlimited possibilities so always consider options beyond a solid wall color. That might mean striping the walls with paint or brushing one hue on the windows and a coordinating color on the window frame. Use lemony-yellow paint to make a dark room bright, vertical stripes to make a short room look higher, and a warm tone to up the visual temperature in a north-facing space.

## THE TECHNIQUES:

For more about painting, see "Surfaces and how to paint them," beginning on page 178.

## THE PALETTE:

Sources, page 187

**AVON GREEN**            **YELLOW**

# Family industry

## THE QUESTION:

*We covered our basement walls with corrugated metal to give it an industrial feel. Do we have to use warm colors to contrast with the cool metal?*

## THE ANSWER:

The cool gray of metal can leave a basement family room feeling a bit chilly. Warm it up with natural wood and add serenity with shades of purple and green.

## THE LESSONS:

• A family room for adults functions as a place to relax after a hard day of work and a movie theater for the weekend. To give the space a relaxed feeling, choose cool or passive colors such as green and purple. These colors calm and restore.

• Shop the market for new kinds of paint such as chalkboard paint to create mini blackboards, paint pens to embellish plain pillows, and concrete paint that sticks tight to floors. Some of the new paints available in paint and crafts stores, such as magnetic paint, can inspire ideas for projects or help you achieve the projects you've already dreamed up. The endless number of colors lets you achieve exactly the look you want.

• Divide a large basement room into several areas anchored by furniture but paint the entire floor the same so you can move the furniture whenever you please. A sectional provides seating by the television, and a desk area tucks into the back corner.

## THE TECHNIQUES:

For more about painting concrete, see "Surfaces and how to paint them," beginning on page 178.

## THE PALETTE:

Sources, page 187

**SASSY GREEN**

**KIWI**

**PLAID PETUNIA**

*Rev up the style in a basement family room by painting the floor in a happy shade of green.*

138

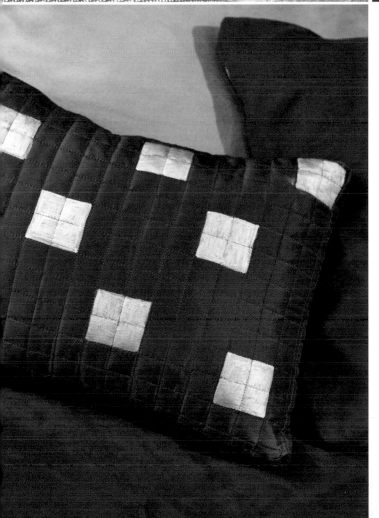

Opposite:
Chalkboard paint on two of the wood wall panels creates a space for instant messaging.

Above left:
Repetition is good for a room, so add painted squares to burlap curtain panels to play up the wood wall squares.

Left:
A quilted pillow provides the pattern for silver squares created using a paint pen.

Above right:
Create a dramatic focal point by painting oversize vessels in bright shades of the purples and greens used in the room. Add metallic accents.

# CHAPTER 10

# Accessories

Small painted projects make perfect starter material even if you have lots of experience with brushes, glazes, and spray cans. After all, small projects let you experiment with new paints, try interesting techniques, or kick off a whole-house makeover by painting an accessory for one room. Some of these products are so much fun to use and deliver such interesting results that you'll soon be painting lampshades, frames, plates, and pillows for every room in your house. Ready to relax this weekend? Pick up a paintbrush and lose yourself in a project.

Have fun with paint:

# Metal chandelier

## THE QUESTION:

How can I update an old rusty chandelier I found at a flea market?

## THE ANSWER:

A bright finish can transport a chandelier from the previous century to this one.

## THE TECHNIQUES:

• Strip off metal parts and wiring to reveal the basic chandelier shape. Using a wire brush, scrub away dirt and rust. Wash and wipe dry.

• Spray the surface with a rust-inhibiting primer; let dry. As with all spray paints, hold the can 8 to 10 inches from the object and apply several light coats to prevent paint runs.

• Spray the chandelier with several light coats of glossy aluminum paint; let dry. You'll find many paints with finishes that look almost as good as metal. Slip glass votive holders into the chandelier parts that once held bulb sockets.

## THE PALETTE:

Sources, page 188

**CHROME**

# Glass lamp base

## THE QUESTION:

*I love the look of mercury-glass lamp bases. Can I do this at home?*

## THE ANSWER:

A new spray product turns clear glass into mirrored glass that looks deceptively like the real thing.

## THE TECHNIQUES:

• For a mirrored effect, you must paint the reverse side of the project. That means you'll need to find a glass lamp base with an open bottom that allows access for spray paint.

• Spray paint can fly everywhere, so use painter's tape and plastic sheeting to cover up the entire exterior surface of the lamp. Wash and dry the glass surface.

• Apply the paint in five very thin coats, spraying 8 to 10 inches from the surface and allowing at least 1 minute between coats. The inside you're painting will look dull, but you'll see the mirror effect when you look at the exterior of the project.

• Wait at least 15 minutes after the last coat and apply clear protective finish to prevent scratching and chipping. The painted area cannot be washed.

## THE PALETTE:

Sources, page 188

**MIRROR**

# Glazed baskets

## THE QUESTION:

*All I can find are baskets painted white or in natural colors. Can I paint rattan?*

## THE ANSWER:

Rattan takes to paint and glazing thanks to its interesting texture.

## THE TECHNIQUES:

• Before you start painting, evaluate the surface. Shiny finishes should be sanded lightly. All surfaces should be primed first with a primer tinted to match the top coat.

• For this finish, apply the base coat of pink using spray paint. This ensures that the paint will seep into every bit of the surface; let dry. To give the basket an aged effect, thin the gray paint 1:1 with glazing liquid. Glazing liquid slows the drying time of paint and gives you more time to perfect the surface treatment. Brush the surface with the paint-glazing-liquid mixture. Immediately use a cotton rag to wipe off the mixture, revealing as much of the pink as you want to see; let dry.

• Seal the surface with a coat or two of clear spray sealer.

## THE PALETTE:

Sources, page 188

**MASONRY GRAY**

**JACARANDA PINK**

# Stencil plates

## THE QUESTION:

*I'm not a skilled painter. Can I really paint china?*

## THE ANSWER:

Pair paint made for slick surfaces with stencils and you'll discover how easy it is to create your own decorative plates.

## THE TECHNIQUES:

• Many paints stick tight to glass and ceramic surfaces. Select the products depending on how you plan to use the painted item and whether it will come in contact with food. Carefully read the paint label before you make a purchase.

• Prepare the surface following the manufacturer's instructions. This may involve a clear primer or surface conditioner.

• To use a stencil, spray the back of the stencil with stencil adhesive and adhere it to the plate. Paint the surface using a small amount of paint and a foam stencil brush; remove stencil and let paint dry.

• Follow the manufacturer's instructions for curing the paint. Some require baking the painted piece in the oven for the paint to become permanent. Although the paint manufacturer may state that the paint is suitable for the dishwasher after baking, it is a good idea to gently wash by hand if possible.

## THE PALETTE:

Sources, page 188

**MEDITERRANEAN**

# Mirror matting

## THE QUESTION:

I saw mirrored mats on framed lithographs in an expensive shop. How can I get this look on a budget?

## THE ANSWER:

The same new product that gave the lamp base (page 145) the look of mercury glass duplicates the look of mirrored mats.

## THE TECHNIQUES:

• Purchase a special mirror-look paint and a picture frame with a glass insert to protect the framed piece. To create this mirrored matting, remove the glass from the frame. Cut paper or stencil plastic sheeting the size and shape of the item you want to frame. The border around the paper or plastic shape will look like mirror after the paint treatment. Spray the paper or plastic with stencil adhesive and stick it to the reverse side of the glass.

• To do several frames, lay all the glass pieces on newspaper outside. Wash and dry the glass surface before painting.

• Apply paint in five very thin coats, spraying 8 to 10 inches from the surface and allowing at least 1 minute between coats. The side you're painting will look dull, but you'll see the mirror effect when you reverse the glass.

• Wait at least 15 minutes after the last coat and apply a clear protective finish to prevent scratching and chipping. Remove the paper or plastic from the center of the glass and reassemble the frames. The painted area cannot be washed.

## THE PALETTE:

Sources, page 188

**MIRROR**

# Striped canisters

## THE QUESTION:

*I found some fun glass canisters for my kitchen. Can I paint them if I plan to use them for food?*

## THE ANSWER:

Check labels carefully if you plan to use paint around food. Most paints are OK to use on the outside of food containers.

## THE TECHNIQUES:

• When painting cylinders, use masking tape that stretches so you can easily wrap the tape around curves. If you can't find this tape, consider stretchable automotive tapes.

• Think through the masking process. For a reverse pattern with frosted stripes, cover up all of the glass you want to remain clear. Make sure you burnish tape edges to keep paint from seeping underneath.

• Spray-paint the surface using several light coats. Remove the masking tape.

## THE PALETTE:

Sources, page 188

**PEARL FROSTED**

# Stamped tablecloth

## THE QUESTION:

*Can I apply paint to my own washable table linens?*

## THE ANSWER:

The market is filled with paints for fabrics that stand up to washing and drying. Buy ready-made table linens or make your own; add painted designs to either.

## THE TECHNIQUES:

• Always follow the specific directions for the paints you purchase. Experiment with stamping techniques on a scrap of fabric placed on top of plastic sheeting. Imperfections created when stamping a design on 100 percent cotton or linen add to the charm.

• Wash, dry, and iron the tablecloth; do not use detergent or fabric softener. Place plastic sheeting on the work surface and lay the tablecloth flat on top.

• Plan the placement of the stamped designs. Mark the locations using a disappearing-ink pen. To coat the stamp with paint, brush or roll a light coating over the surface, taking care to prevent paint from building up in the indentations of the stamp. First press the stamp on a paper towel to remove some of the paint, then on a fabric scrap to test your technique. Be sure to lift the stamp straight up to avoid smudging the paint. When you're happy with the look, repeat the same process on the tablecloth.

## THE PALETTE:

Sources, page 188

**BUTTERSCOTCH**

How To Paint Just About Anything

# Painted lampshades

## THE QUESTION:

*Paper lampshades are so inexpensive I'm going to make a set for every season. Any new products I should try?*

## THE ANSWER:

Spray paints work best on paper, so choose from a variety of fun finishes such as suede, metal, and stone.

## THE TECHNIQUES:

• The most difficult and time-consuming part of this project will be setting up an area in which to paint. In good weather you might want to suspend the shades from a tree branch away from any surfaces the paint might damage. Or create a spray booth using a large box and hang the shades from string taped to the top of the box.

• Spray lightly and repeatedly for the most even coverage.

## THE PALETTE:

Sources, page 188

**CHARCOAL SANDSTONE**

**SILVER METALLIC**

# Vinyl roller shade

## THE QUESTION:

My new house has vinyl roller shades on every window. How can I give them some much-needed personality?

## THE ANSWER:

Combine a variety of paint colors and use painter's tape, stamps, and stencils to add personality to these generic window coverings.

## THE TECHNIQUES:

• Select from room-darkening or light-filtering shades. Paint will appear opaque on the room-darkening shades while light will add an interesting effect to paint on light-filtering shades.

• To create this layered stripe-and-stencil pattern, use painter's tape to make wide stripes. Paint between tape edges using a small foam paint roller; remove tape and let dry.

• To paint the stencil pattern, apply stencil adhesive to the back of the stencil and lay it in place on the shade. Dip a foam roller in paint and roll it over newspaper until the roller leaves only a light coating of paint; roll over the stencil. If your roller is too full of paint, the paint will bleed under the stencil. Remove the stencil; let paint dry. Move the stencil to the next spot and repeat the process until the shade is covered.

## THE PALETTE:

Sources, page 188

JACARANDA PINK

EDGECOMB GRAY

# Plastic urn

## THE QUESTION:

*I love the shape of plastic urns, but I want a hammered-metal finish. Can I do that?*

## THE ANSWER:

Try one of the hammered metal spray paints. They're easy to apply and stand up to weather.

## THE TECHNIQUES:

• Wash plastic surface; let dry.

• For even coverage, protect a fence post with a drop cloth. Set the urn on top and apply three or four light coats of hammered-metal spray. It's best to use this paint in a well-ventilated area. The paint will produce a textured surface that covers up any plastic seams or other irregularities. Make sure you paint the top 3 or 4 inches inside of the urn if you plan to plant it. If you're using the urn as a decorative container, paint the entire inside surface.

## THE PALETTE:

Sources, page 188

**SILVER HAMMERED**

# Silvered wood frame

## THE QUESTION:

*I'd love to display my favorite photos in a collection of silver frames, but all of my frames are wood. Can I make them look like silver?*

## THE ANSWER:

Metallic finishes today really look like metal. That's because some of these paints contain real metal particles that will tarnish naturally over time and others contain particles that mimic the look of metal. So transform those wood frames with a metal finish such as the sterling-silver paint shown here.

## THE TECHNIQUES:

• Prepare the surface. Sand slick surfaces and wash all surfaces to remove dust and oils; allow to dry.

• Follow the directions on the product you've chosen. Products are packaged in a variety of sizes from ounces to gallons. Most of these paints require a primer coat before top-coating the metal on the surface. Look for spray and brush-on metal paints and choose the version that's right for your project.

## THE PALETTE:

Sources, page 188

**STERLING SILVER**

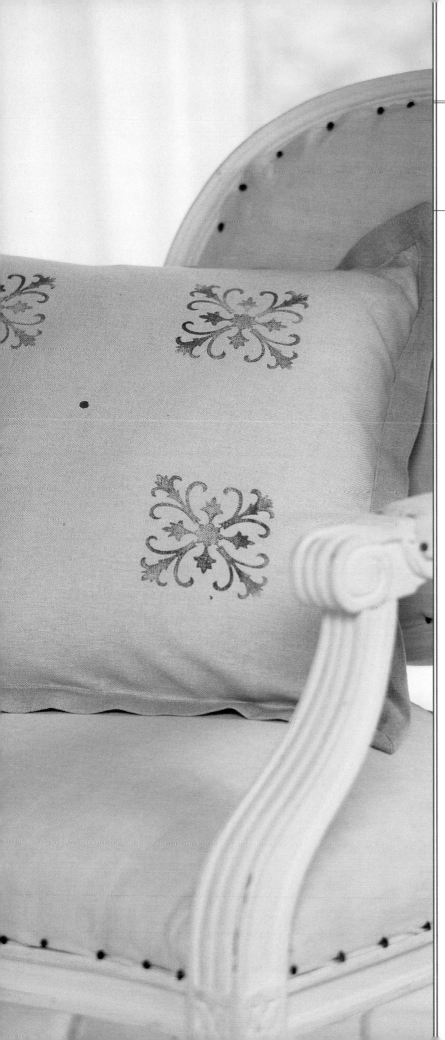

# Stamped pillow top

## THE QUESTION:

I can't sew so I have to buy pillows off the rack. How can I give them a bit of my style in the colors I love?

## THE ANSWER:

The possibilities are endless using fabric paint or regular paint mixed with textile medium, and stamps, stencils, or freehand designs.

## THE TECHNIQUES:

• Always experiment with your techniques on a scrap of fabric on top of plastic sheeting. Most paints work best on 100 percent cotton or linen. The imperfections that naturally occur as you stamp a design on fabric give the piece character and charm.

• Remove the pillow form. Wash, dry, and iron the pillow cover; do not use detergent or fabric softener. Line the inside of the pillow cover with a plastic garbage bag to keep paint from bleeding through to the back.

• Determine the placement of the stamped designs and mark them using a disappearing-ink pen. Brush or roll a light coating of paint on the stamp pad; blot on a paper towel to remove some of the paint. Press the stamp on a scrap of fabric to check your technique; lift the stamp straight up to avoid smudging the paint. When you're happy with the look, repeat the same process on the pillow cover.

• To use a stencil instead of a stamp, cut the stencil from self-adhesive vinyl (the kind used for shelf liners). If using a ready-made plastic stencil, apply spray adhesive to the back to temporarily adhere it to the fabric.

## THE PALETTE:

Sources, page 188

**MEDITERRANEAN**

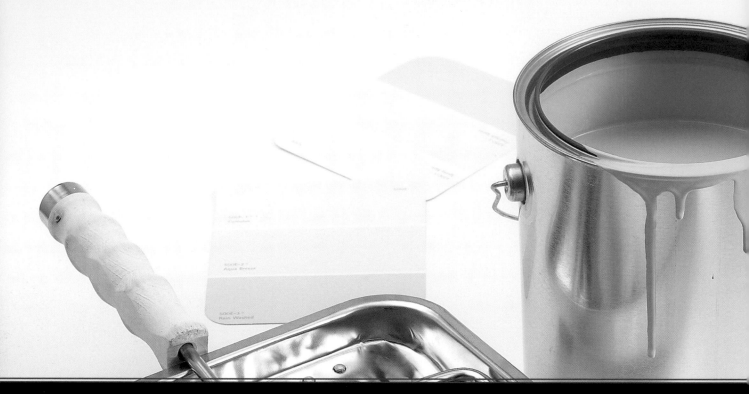

# CHAPTER 11

# Outdoors

Paints for use outdoors have to be tough, and they are. They last through sun, rain, snow, freezing lows, blistering highs, neglect, and abuse. Newer finishes on the market promise longer color retention and better surface adhesion. Some products, such as paint for plastic, tackle old problems with easy new solutions. Metal paints endure against rust and eliminate the need for primer. Even 2-ounce bottles of crafts paints are formulated for use on metals and plastic. So give your outdoor spaces the same attention and painted finishes you once reserved for indoors. We guarantee you'll be spending more time in the fresh air once the paint dries.

Paints for outdoors:
- Outdoor stencil paint, page 161
- Metal finishes for wood, page 161
- Rust-inhibiting paint, page 164
- Concrete paint, page 166
- Paint for plastic, page 169

Dining in view of the garden promises the ultimate in simplicity and sophistication.

# Dine alfresco

## THE QUESTION:

*Summer evenings are so delightful we'd like to use our garden for entertaining. A standard picnic table doesn't seem dressy enough. Can I give some everyday pieces a dressed-up attitude using paint?*

## THE ANSWER:

Paint is the great chameleon of the design world. It can make things look bigger, smaller, older, newer, and, in the case of your outdoor table, even dressier.

## THE LESSONS:

• A neutral palette in the garden strikes the right note if you want a dressy attitude. By limiting colors to white and silver, you elevate the garden greens and flower hues to star status. Seasonal flowers change the look. Just imagine pale violet in spring, hot pink in midsummer, and orange in fall.

• When you're creating an outdoor "room," eliminate the indoor and outdoor labels and just imagine a space filled with the things you love. That will ensure a look that suits your style sensibilities. Approach the finishing of the pieces the same way to ensure that the effect is spectacular rather than predictable.

• Always make sure the products you use will stand up to the weather. Note, too, that paints come in a variety of sizes, as small as 2-ounce bottles and 3-ounce spray cans.

## THE TECHNIQUES:

For more about painting plastic and glass, see "Surfaces and how to paint them," beginning on page 178.

## THE PALETTE:

Sources, page 188

**SILVER STERLING**

**ALUMINUM**

**PEARL FROSTED GLASS**

A long, narrow table has space for four to eight diners. Add chairs as needed but store chairs between meals.

Above left:
Silver paint makes a wood tabletop look like stainless steel.

Above right:
A primitive urn and leaf pattern adds a touch of the past to laminate chairs.

Left:
Votives sprayed with a frosted glass finish suspend light above the table.

# Color confidence

## THE QUESTION:

*Everything in my garden is white. I'd like to try a color but need a little advice. Any foolproof garden hues?*

## THE ANSWER:

White has its place in the garden, but so do lots of other shades. Here's a look at one color that's perfect with green.

## THE LESSONS:

• Blue-purple looks so good in the garden because it creates a complementary color scheme with the greens of grass, leaves, and flowers. Complementary colors look more intense side by side than they do on their own. Green, of course, dominates, which is the perfect way to create a complementary palette.

• Unstructured gardens with rambling flower beds and blowsy blooms offer perfect backgrounds for painted finishes, such as this plaid, which intentionally looks hand-painted. To support the palette, bring a little yellow-green to the chair surface.

• A white-painted arbor shouts, "Look at me!" When painted purple, the arbor recedes and makes the path and flowers along it seem more important. Paint with an exterior paint over an exterior primer tinted to match the top coat.

## THE TECHNIQUES:

For more about painting wood and metal, see "Surfaces and how to paint them," beginning on page 178.

## THE PALETTE:

Sources, page 188

**COBALT GLAZE**

**MAGENTA**

**CAROLINA PARAKEET**

**AWARD BLUE**

*Below:*
*An arbor painted purple provides a destination and vista for a garden.*

*Opposite:*
*Metal chairs from the 1950s, found on a garbage heap, sport a colorful new finish.*

# Fresh-air living

## THE QUESTION:

My front porch is filled with flea market finds, but nothing goes together. Where do I start?

## THE ANSWER:

Spray paints are the perfect answer for painting everything outdoors, from lawn chairs to flowerpots. Because the colors of spray paints are limited, shop first, then decide on your color scheme.

## THE LESSONS:

• Always buy pieces based on shape; use paint to make them feel like a cohesive grouping. It's easy to paint almost any surface, so pick chairs with the right curve to the back and plastic flowerpots that will look stately with a new finish.

• Spray paints are easy to apply if you remember to spray many thin coats so the paint won't build up and run. Use a rust-inhibiting spray paint for metal, texture spray paints to cover worn surfaces, and spray paint for glass to create accessories. Aluminum paint covers the vintage lawn chairs while spray paint in a suede or stone finish disguises plastic pots.

• Let a favorite fabric, such as the ticking on the cushions, determine the palette. The ticking inspired the scheme of taupe, gray, and a touch of blue on the sisal rug. Create the pattern for the rug using painter's tape.

## THE TECHNIQUES:

For more about new paints, see "Special Paints" on page 185.

## THE PALETTE:

Sources, page 188

**ALUMINUM**

**COBALT**

**BUCKSKIN SUEDE**

**CHARCOAL SAND STONE**

Above:
One end of a long front porch makes space for summertime lounging.

Left:
Cushions on the chairs and a painted rug underfoot make this outdoor room feel as comfortable as indoors.

Opposite top:
A glass vase ringed with glass paint and inverted serves as a cloche over a moss plant.

Opposite middle:
Spray-on finishes—stone in gray and suede in taupe— take only a few minutes.

Opposite bottom:
Stripes on the rug repeat the pattern of the ticking cushions on the chairs.

Dress up a boring concrete
patio with a painted "rug."
For fun, add a fringe of
stenciled forks.

How To Paint Just About Anything

Two coats of concrete paint provide the base for the painted pattern, while an exterior sealer protects it from wear.

# Sitting pretty

## THE QUESTION:

Our concrete patio looks dingy and stained. Can I paint it?

## THE ANSWER:

Concrete paint provides a new surface you can roll on in a weekend. It also provides a base to create your own outdoor "rug."

## THE LESSONS:

• Pick your favorite colors for use outdoors. Almost any combination will work, but the most effective palettes include a shade or two of green. If your garden is visible from the patio, include some of the colors of the flowers you grow.

• Although painting the design is the fun part, you'll need to start and end with some specific steps to preserve your work. The first step is to wash the concrete with a solution of muriatic acid. Look for it in home centers, and carefully follow the directions when working with this caustic product. Once the concrete is etched, follow with two coats of concrete paint suitable for use outdoors. Protect the surface with an exterior sealer.

• It's easy to be playful with design outside because you don't have to worry about adjoining rooms or whole-house color schemes. Look for stencil patterns of vegetables, scrolls, and forks to create a rug that's similar to this one. You might even let your children create the rug design. After all, it's easy to paint over in a few years if your style changes.

## THE TECHNIQUES:

For more about painting concrete, see "Surfaces and how to paint them," beginning on page 178.

## THE PALETTE:

Sources, page 188

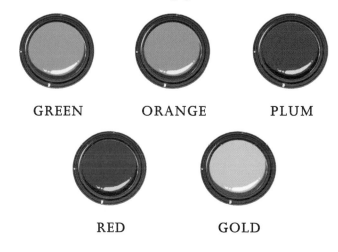

GREEN     ORANGE     PLUM

RED     GOLD

# Sun spots

## THE QUESTION:

How can I create a getaway spot just for me in my backyard that's stylish but doesn't dip into my vacation savings?

## THE ANSWER:

Start with an inexpensive plastic chaise and give it a designer look with spray paint for plastic. Painted dots dress up a basic outdoor umbrella. And rust-inhibiting paint is just the thing for turning an old metal stool into a weather-worthy end table.

## THE LESSONS:

• A garden umbrella is as perfect for hiding you from the neighbors as it is for blocking unwanted sun. But before you prop it between you and the view you want to block, give it some design pizzazz. Use outdoors crafts paints and paint freehand or use a stencil for circles with crisp edges. You'll love how the pattern shows from both sides.

• Plastic lawn furniture has a lot going for it—low price, easy to move, and comfortable—but it doesn't earn many points for style. That changes when you spray the surface with a fun new finish such as silver metallic paint. It turns plastic into designer silver and takes only an hour or so to do. Just be careful to apply several light coats so the paint doesn't run.

• Add comfort with a purchased pillow decorated with a flower stencil. The pillow collects the color palette all in one spot. Cut stencils from self-adhesive shelf liner. It clings to fabric while you paint and removes easily. Just make sure you line the pillow cover with plastic before you stencil.

## THE TECHNIQUES:

For more about painting fabric, see "Surfaces and how to paint them," beginning on page 178.

## THE PALETTE:

Sources, page 188

**PEWTER GRAY**        **FRESH FOLIAGE**

Hide away under a painted umbrella when a day at the beach won't fit your schedule.

Above:
Because fabric is translucent, the painted pattern shows through the underside of the umbrella.

Opposite top:
Spray paint in metallic silver updates a plastic chaise.

Opposite middle:
A flea market metal table looks brand new with a coat of rust-inhibiting paint.

Opposite bottom:
Paint dots freehand for a casual look or use a stencil for crisp edges.

# Street signs

## THE QUESTION:

How can I make a statement with my house numbers? Most of the ones I can afford are too small and too boring.

## THE ANSWER:

Think big. Give your house numbers the importance they deserve with these bold ideas. No one will have trouble finding your house ever again.

## THE LESSONS:

• Oversize numbers and letters have been popping up everywhere in interior design. Bring that same attitude to the numbers in your address with this fun fair-weather idea. Use outdoor crafts paint to create big numbers on premade throw pillows; toss them on the porch bench next to your front door. You can create a similar effect by painting your house numbers on a banner to hang by your front door.

• Announce your address at the front gate with 2-foot-tall letters cut from plywood. They'll look like hammered metal once you spray them with shiny metal paint that's suitable for exterior use. Or try a spray finish that looks like hammered aluminum or copper.

• Search in a secondhand store or flea market for old metal house numbers. To give them a fresh new coat, try one of the metal spray paints that protects against rust.

## THE TECHNIQUES:

For more about paints for outdoors, see "Special Paints" on page 185.

## THE PALETTE:

Sources, page 188

**CHROME**

**BLACK**

*Above:*
*Spray metal paint*
*gives plywood letters*
*the look of metal.*

House numbers painted on pillows sit by the front door.

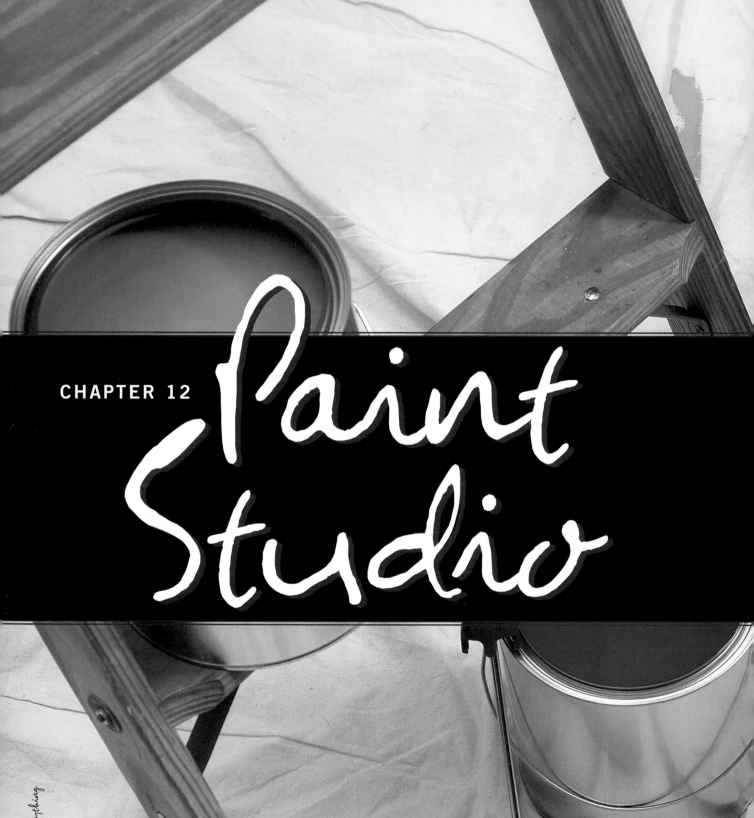

# CHAPTER 12

# Paint Studio

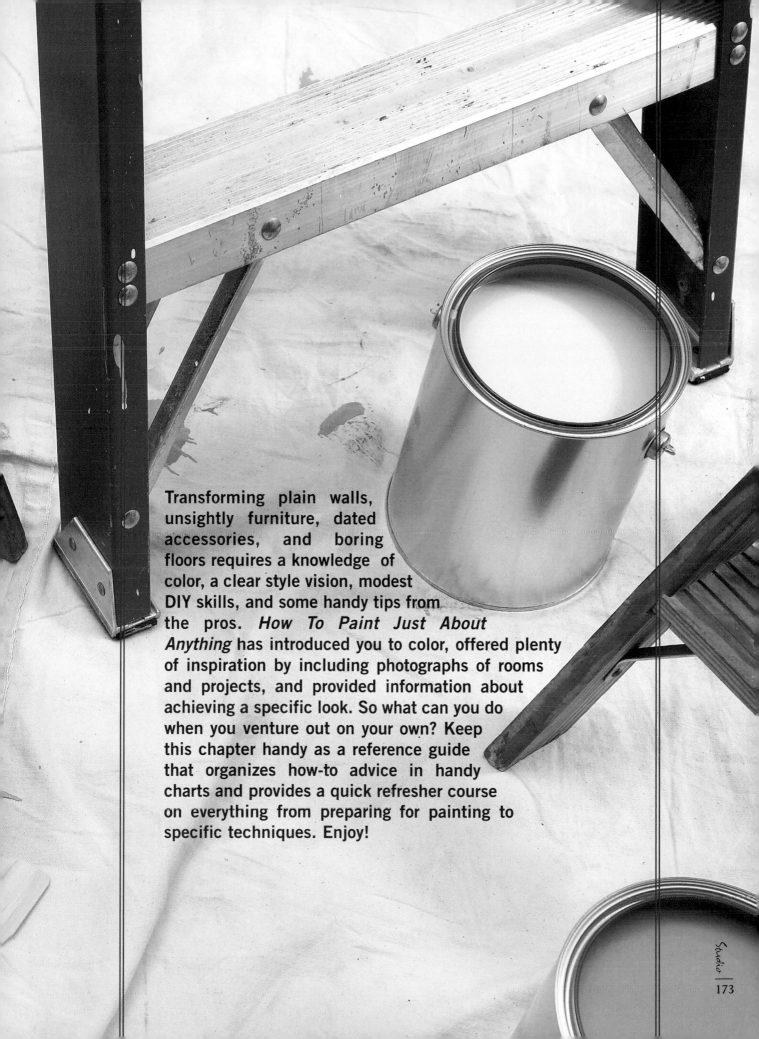

Transforming plain walls, unsightly furniture, dated accessories, and boring floors requires a knowledge of color, a clear style vision, modest DIY skills, and some handy tips from the pros. *How To Paint Just About Anything* has introduced you to color, offered plenty of inspiration by including photographs of rooms and projects, and provided information about achieving a specific look. So what can you do when you venture out on your own? Keep this chapter handy as a reference guide that organizes how-to advice in handy charts and provides a quick refresher course on everything from preparing for painting to specific techniques. Enjoy!

# All the gear for painting

**Ready to spread some paint? Start with the right supplies.**

## BRUSH BASICS

Buy good-quality, synthetic-bristle brushes because they hold more paint, retain their bristles, and provide a tapered edge that makes it easy to apply paint. Use only synthetic-bristle brushes with latex paint and natural-fiber or synthetic brushes with alkyd paint. Buy small angled brushes for windows, larger angled brushes to edge around woodwork, and large flat brushes for big projects. Store brushes in their original packaging to help the bristles maintain their shape.

TIP: To test brush quality, tug on the brush. If more than two bristles come out, it's poorly constructed.

Brushes from left:

• 2-inch angled brushes: Use for painting narrow areas near molding. The shaped bristles make it easy to paint clean edges against trim and along the edge between the wall and ceiling. Hold these brushes like a pencil.

• 1-inch angled brush: Perfect for painting mullions and picture frames.

• 3-inch flat brush: Use this brush to outline walls and ceilings, a technique known as "cutting in."

## ROLLER BASICS

Use short-nap rollers for smooth surfaces and long-nap rollers for rough surfaces. Test the quality of a roller by squeezing it. A good roller will quickly return to its original shape. If you separate the nap on the roller cover, you shouldn't be able to see its cardboard core. Also, as with brushes, use synthetic rollers for water-base paint and synthetic or natural-fiber rollers for alkyd paint. Select the width of the roller depending on the size of the project.

TIP: Short nap rollers leave less paint on the surface, which may require an additional coat.

Rollers from left:

• Short-nap roller cover (yellow): Use short-nap roller covers for smooth surfaces and smooth finishes.

• Long-nap roller cover (orange): Use to cover rough surfaces. The roller leaves a slight texture.

• 4- and 6-inch roller covers: Use them to squeeze into narrow spaces between windows and doors and to efficiently paint furniture. Small foam rollers make short work of wall and floor stenciling.

## INDISPENSABLE TOOL

Pick up the aptly named painter's tool at any hardware store or home center. Look for variations that promise six to 13 tasks. Here's some of what it can do:

• Poke holes in paint can rims when you tap its pointed end with a rubber mallet or hammer, *right*. These holes allow excess paint to drip back inside after pouring.

• Act as a putty knife to apply surfacing compound to nail holes and gouges.

• Open paint cans with its flat edge.

• Scrape excess paint from a roller with the curved portion, *right*.

• Unstick painted-over windows when run along the sashes' edges.

## PAINTER'S TAPE

For protecting surfaces from paint, use a low-tack quick-release tape, called painter's tape, along moldings, around windows, and to cover up any parts that won't be painted. The tape comes in a variety of sizes. Although it is more expensive than regular masking tape, it won't leave a sticky residue and it removes cleanly. This product works perfectly when used to create geometric painted patterns on walls, floors, and furniture.

## TO PRIME OR NOT?

Take the guesswork out of your decision.

• Primer is necessary only on new or weathered wood or other raw surfaces, on an uneven or deteriorated painted surface, or on a stripped surface.

• Professional painters like to use tinted primers when repainting walls using contrasting colors. For best coverage, have primer tinted the same color as the paint that will be painted over it. Primers are richer in resins than ordinary paint so they provide a better base for a final finish.

• Primers and sealers come in latex (water-base) and alkyd formulations. If your paint is water-base, your primer must be water-base. If your paint is alkyd, the primer can be water-base or alkyd.

• Look for primers that block stains, prime drywall or plaster, block rust on metal objects, or cling tight to shiny surfaces.

• If the surfaces to be painted have ink and crayon marks or water stains, use a stain-blocking primer prior to painting. This will prevent marks and stains from bleeding through the finished paint.

## HOW TO PICK PAINT

Paints are not created equal. Premium paints, whether water-base or alkyd, contain more paint solids (pigments and binders) and less liquid. They are more durable, adhesive, fade-resistant, and uniform in color and sheen, and often require fewer coats for complete coverage. Premium paints are a better long-term investment because they generally require repainting in 10 years instead of 4 years with less-expensive paint.

### LATEX OR WATER-BASE PAINTS

Low-odor, fast-drying latex paints have a water base (quality paints have no more than 50 percent water content) and account for the majority of paint sold. Compared with alkyd paints, the color in latex paint is less likely to fade, chalk, crack, or grow mildew. New advances in paint manufacturing have made latex paints as adhesive as and longer lasting than alkyd. These paints resist cracking and chipping better than alkyd paints. Besides general interior painting, latex is the best choice for exterior wood, new stucco and masonry, or weathered aluminum and vinyl siding.

### ALKYD OR OIL-BASE PAINTS

These paints are made of petroleum distillates, pigments, and resins; most of the liquid portion is petroleum solvent. The best paints have no more than 30 percent solvent. Oil-base paint has excellent adhesion and fair durability, but it's more likely to harden, become brittle, and yellow over time. It has a strong odor, and must be cleaned with mineral spirits, and its drying time is long (from 8 to 24 hours). Alkyd paint is your best choice when you repaint a surface with four or more layers of old oil-base paint. Do not use alkyd paint on fresh masonry or galvanized iron because the paint will fail quickly.

TIP: You can paint latex over alkyd, but avoid painting alkyd over latex. The latex layer underneath is flexible and will expand and contract, causing an alkyd top coat to crack. To test which paint you have, rub mineral spirits on the surface; alkyd will generally dissolve, whereas latex will be unaffected.

## HOW MUCH PAINT DO YOU NEED?

• Measure lengths of all walls you plan to paint; multiply the total by the floor-to-ceiling height to get square footage.

• Subtract 20 square feet for each door and 15 square feet for each window.

• Divide the result by the spreading rate of the paint (shown on the label; usually 400 square feet per gallon) to figure the gallons needed. Or use an online paint calculator at one of the paint manufacturers' websites.

# Prepping for the job

Getting a room ready to paint will likely take longer than actually painting it but preparation is key to a professional-looking job. Plan on one to three hours of prep time for every hour spent painting. That's because paint is a liquid that conforms to the surface, and if the surface is rough or uneven, the finished look will be rough and uneven.

## GETTING READY TO PAINT

1. An empty room is easy to paint. Remove breakable items, such as accessories, take down everything from the walls, and move the furniture to the center of the room and cover it with drop cloths to protect it from paint spatters. Cover the floors with drop cloths.

2. Turn off power to any outlet or fixture you will be painting. Remove outlet and switchplate covers; put a piece of painter's tape over the outlet box. Tape the screws to the backs of the covers and slide the covers into a plastic bag to keep them together; tape the bag to a window in the room. Remove heat registers and drapery hardware. Loosen the canopy of any ceiling fixture and slide it away from the ceiling. Wrap the canopy and doorknobs in plastic wrap secured with rubber bands.

3. Put a lined trash can in the middle of the room so you can dispose of trash as it accumulates.

4. Clean up dirt and grease spots using TSP (trisodium phosphate), a nonsudsing cleaner. No rinsing needed.

5. Repair surface problems such as cracks, dings, and small holes. Hold a work light at a low angle against the walls to throw surface imperfections into sharp relief.

6. Clean up after repairs. Vacuum the floor, molding, and walls. Wipe down moldings with a tack rag.

7. Tape off areas you don't want painted using painter's tape. Blue tape is designed for use with latex paints and other water-base finishes. Purple tape is for alkyd finishes. Both stay on regardless of humidity and stick for at least seven days. Their real benefit is that they come off without causing damage. Though many professional painters don't mask-off areas, their practiced hands are steadier than the average painter's. You might feel  safer protecting these items. Make sure you run a tapered plastic tool along the edge to complete the seal. Peel quick-release tape off as soon as you're done painting so you can wipe off paint smears while they're still wet.

8. Prime even if walls were previously painted. Primer maximizes coverage and delivers a uniform finish.

## TIPS FOR FIXING DINGS, DENTS, AND CRACKS

Try these strategies for repairing common plaster and drywall problems.

**• Small surface dings in drywall or plaster**
Sand surface with 80-grit sandpaper. Fill dings with lightweight surfacing compound; let dry. Sand. Prime to ensure even coverage of the top coat. Try one of the new surfacing compounds that are pink when applied and white when dry.

**• Small holes in wood**
Fill holes with interior patching compound. Sand the patched areas first using 180-grit paper; lightly sand the entire surface. Clean up dust with a tack rag.

**• Cracks in plaster**
Undercut cracks wider than ¼ inch to make them broader at the bottom; this helps lock in the filler material. Blow out any loose plaster. Wet the crack with a sponge and pack compound into it with a putty knife. Use patching plaster to fill large holes and cracks. After 24 hours, wet the area again with a sponge and level off with a coat of patching material. When dry, sand and prime with two coats of white-pigmented sealer.

**• Holes in drywall**
Clean out debris and sand lightly. Pack the dent with lightweight spackling compound. Let dry; sand. For large holes, bridge the hole with a piece of fiberglass tape; apply joint compound. Let dry overnight then sand with 150-grit sandpaper or smooth with a damp sponge. With a 6-inch broad knife, apply vinyl surfacing compound using horizontal and vertical sweeps; let dry. Sand with 120-grit sandpaper. Seal with two coats of white-pigmented sealer.

**• Flaking or peeling spots**
Flaky, peeling spots can indicate that oil-base paint turned brittle or the original surface may not have been properly dulled or cleaned, causing poor paint adhesion. Scrape off loose paint, then sand.

**• Wallpaper**
It is usually best to remove wallpaper before painting. Try a gel stripper or make your own stripping solution by mixing 1 part vinegar in 1 part water. Put in a spray bottle and spray onto the wallpaper; peel or scrape away.

WARNING:
Paint that is older than 20 years may contain lead. If you suspect the old paint contains lead, never sand it and try not to disturb it. Contact a local paint retailer about how to proceed.

## STEP-BY-STEP TO A PERFECT FINISH

• Always provide adequate ventilation for painting. Depending on the kind of paint you're using and your own tolerance, you may want to wear a dust mask and goggles to prevent lung and eye irritation.

• Stir the paint. If you've just arrived home from buying the paint, you can omit this step. If you've waited a few days, use a stir stick to make sure the heavier pigmented material that settles is mixed in with the liquid.

• Paint the ceiling before the walls. Edge first, and then paint the ceiling with a roller and an extension handle to avoid standing on a ladder.

• Load a brush by dipping one-third of its bristles into paint. Lift the bristles out of the paint, and gently tap (don't wipe) them against the can's rim (photo 1).

• Holding a brush correctly, like a pencil, is one of the keys to successful painting and reduction of hand fatigue (photo 2).

• For a clean edge use an angle-bristle brush when cutting in. Leave a loosely brushed edge that allows the trimmed portion to blend in when you paint the wall (photo 3). A crisp line will be more visible—and more difficult to cover.

• Fill in the outlined areas on the walls using a roller. Dampen the roller; dip it into a paint tray, and roll it up the tray's ramp until the cover is saturated, but not dripping. Paint strokes in a W pattern for even coverage (photo 4). Once a wall is covered with diagonal strokes, use long floor-to-ceiling strokes to fill in any uncovered areas. As you roll, overlap still-wet areas to prevent roll marks.

• Use plastic paint tray liners. They're inexpensive and make cleanup a snap. These disposable liners can be thrown away after use.

• Use an extension handle to increase your reach (photo 5). These handy tools screw into the roller handle. Some new roller cages come with twist-and-extend handles.

• Take a look at the painted surface after it has dried for 24 hours. Touch up any areas that are not evenly covered.

## NO-FUSS CLEANUP

Protect your investment in good tools by properly cleaning and storing paintbrushes and roller covers.

• Remove as much paint as possible from a brush by drawing a brush comb or wire brush through the bristles and working the bristles back and forth across newspaper.

• If you're using alkyd paint, immerse the brush's bristles in a small jar of solvent or mineral spirits; tilt the handle to bend the bristles back and forth until the solvent clouds up. Change the solvent and repeat until the bristles are clean; wash the brush with dish soap and warm water.

• If you're using latex paint, simply wash the brush under running water, bending the bristles back and forth in the palm of your hand to work out all traces of paint. Always let the water run from the handle down to the bristles, not the other way around.

• To remove excess solvent or water from a roller cover, cut the bottom off a 5-gallon plastic bucket and put the bucket in a sink. Place the cover on a spinner and use the spinner inside the bucket; its sides will catch spatters, right.

# Surfaces and how to paint them

| SURFACE | PRODUCTS | PREPARATION |
|---|---|---|
| **BRICK** | Trisodium phosphate (TSP) cleaner and wire brush<br>High-quality latex primer<br>High-quality latex paint | Scrub bricks with a wire brush to remove dirt and chalk. Thoroughly clean surface with TSP cleaner and a wire brush. |
| **CERAMIC TILE** | TSP cleaner<br>150-grit sandpaper<br>Bonding primer<br>Gloss or semigloss latex paint or paints for ceramic and porcelain surfaces | Sand tiles lightly with 150-grit sandpaper to increase surface adhesion. Wash walls with TSP cleaner to remove dirt and grease. |
| **CHINA** | Surface conditioner<br>Ceramic paints<br>Clear-gloss glaze | Follow the paint manufacturer's guidelines for preparing the surface. This may include washing the item in soapy water or brushing the object with a surface conditioner. |
| **UNPAINTED CONCRETE FLOORS** | Cement or mortar for repairs<br>TSP cleaner<br>Bleach solution<br>Water-base acrylic primer<br>High-quality latex paint | Scrub surface, wash with TSP cleaner, and wipe with bleach solution. Remove loose paint by scraping and sanding. Remove oily spots using a degreasing solution, following the label directions. Allow the surface to dry for several days. Make repairs. Etch the surface using a 10 percent solution of muriatic acid and water. Follow manufacturer's instructions carefully as muriatic acid can cause chemical burns when not handled properly. |
| **CONCRETE BLOCK** | Cement or mortar for repairs<br>TSP cleaner<br>Bleach solution<br>Water-base acrylic primer<br>High-quality latex paint | Wait 60 to 90 days for new concrete and mortar to cure before painting. Use a stiff brush to remove any loose material. Clean out cracks and repair holes with cement or mortar; cure repairs for two weeks before painting. Thoroughly scrub the surface with TSP cleaner. If you notice signs of mold or mildew, wash the wall with a bleach solution (1 cup bleach to 1 gallon of water); let dry for 48 hours before painting. |
| **DRYWALL** | TSP cleaner<br>Lightweight spackling compound<br>Stain-blocking primer<br>Latex paint | Dust walls with a clean dust mop or a vacuum cleaner. Wash walls with TSP cleaner to remove grease and dirt. Scrape off any loose paint, and fill holes with spackling compound. Mask areas you don't want painted. |
| **FABRIC** | Water-base paint<br>Textile medium | Wash fabrics before painting but do not use detergent or fabric softener. Lay fabric on a plastic-covered work surface (line pillow shams with plastic bags). Pull fabric taut and secure with pins to the work surface. |

| PAINTING | CARE | TIP |
|---|---|---|
| Wait 30 days to paint newly installed brick. Prime surface, then paint with a high-quality latex paint. Use a long-nap roller cover to apply the paint and a brush to spread the paint to crevices and grout lines. | Wash with a mild household detergent. | Painting brick is a permanent decision because removing paint from this porous surface causes too much damage. |
| Always test products in a hidden area. Apply a bonding primer or one of the new primers that adheres to shiny surfaces; let dry. For even coverage, paint the grout and tiles rather than attempting to paint just the tiles. Follow manufacturer's instructions. The paint may dry in a few hours, but the tiles are not completely cured for several weeks. Take care not to scratch the paint while it is curing. Note: Some products may not work for ceramic tile in a shower. | Wash with mild household detergent. Do not wash with abrasive cleaners. | Use separate products for painting installed tile versus uninstalled tile that can be slipped into to the oven to set the paint. |
| For small amounts of paint, buy 2-ounce bottles. Shake before use. Use bristle or foam brushes to apply the paint. Let each coat of paint dry before adding the next color to keep colors from blending. Cure the finish following the manufacturer's directions. This may include adding a clear sealer or baking the piece in the oven to set the finish. | Follow the paint manufacturer's directions for washing the dishes. | If you are painting dishes you plan to use for food, make sure the paint is food safe. |
| Use floor paint specially formulated for concrete, such as a water-base acrylic primer and high-quality latex paint. Check the manufacturer's label. Apply two to three coats allowing paint to dry between coats. | Wash with a mild household detergent. | Moisture can cause adhesion failure in paint. Test any paint in an out-of-the-way place before painting the entire floor. If building a new home, install a vapor barrier and gravel underneath the concrete floor to ensure that it stays dry. |
| On unpainted concrete, seal with a masonry sealer. For painted concrete, coat with an acrylic latex primer. Paint using a high-quality latex paint. | Wash as needed with a household detergent. | Many new products on the market address the problems of painting below-grade concrete surfaces. Check with your paint retailer for products that might work in your conditions. Many of these products offer guarantees. |
| Use stain-blocking primer to cover crayon marks, water stains, and deep pigments on previously painted drywall and to prepare new drywall for painting. For easier coverage, have primer tinted the same color as the finish coat. Add mildewcide to paint used in bathrooms and kitchens. Apply several thin coats rather than one thick coat. | Wash first with mild detergent. If stains persist, scrub with a plastic brush and stronger detergent. | Pick the paint sheen to suit its use: semigloss for walls that will require lots of scrubbing and satin for walls that won't. Try one of the new scrubbable matte finishes for a flat finish that promises easy care and offers a designer look. |
| Thin water-base paint with textile medium following manufacturer's directions. Apply to the fabric in several thin coats. | Follow directions on the textile medium for setting the color, such as putting fabric in the clothes dryer. | Test your fabric painting skills on fabric remnants first. |

# Surfaces and how to paint them

| SURFACE | PRODUCTS | PREPARATION |
|---|---|---|
| **GLASS** | Surface conditioner<br>Ceramic paints, stained-glass spray paints, or acrylic enamel glass paints<br>Clear-gloss glaze | Select the paint for the type of project you have in mind. Follow the paint manufacturer's guidelines for preparing the surface. This may include washing the item in soapy water or brushing the object with a surface conditioner. |
| **LAMINATE COUNTERTOPS** | TSP cleaner<br>Primer for nonporous surfaces or acrylic primer<br>Acrylic latex enamel | Sand with 150-grit sandpaper to rough up the surface; remove dust. Wash with TSP cleaner to remove grease and grime. Tape off the edges. |
| **METAL** | Spray primer<br>Spray paint | Clean surface with a wire brush to remove flaking paint. Sand slick surfaces to promote adhesion of the top coat. Wipe the surface with a damp rag; let dry. |
| **NEW PLASTER** | Latex acrylic primer<br>High-quality interior latex paint | Fill any holes. Wipe the surface with a dry rag. |
| **PLASTIC** | TSP cleaner<br>Spray paint for plastic<br>Outdoor acrylic enamel paint | Sand lightly to improve adhesion. Wash surface with TSP cleaner. Take care not to touch the surface after cleaning because you'll leave oils on the surface that will prevent paint adhesion. |
| **VINYL FLOORING** | TSP cleaner<br>Liquid deglosser<br>Latex stain-blocking primer<br>High-quality latex or modified epoxy latex paint<br>Clear polyurethane | Clean the floor with TSP cleaner to remove grease and grime. Sand with 220-grit sandpaper to dull the shine. Wipe clean, and apply a liquid deglosser for better adhesion. |
| **WOOD/PAINTED OR VARNISHED** | Lightweight spackling compound<br>Stain-blocking primer/sealer<br>Self-leveling paint to hide brushstrokes | Remove dirt or wax buildup with a high-strength household cleaner; rinse. Dull the glossy surface with 150-grit sandpaper. Wipe with a damp rag to remove residue. Fill any holes with lightweight spackling compound. |
| **WOOD/ UNFINISHED** | Stain-blocking primer/sealer.<br>Paint<br>Paint extender and conditioner to improve brushability and workability<br>Clear polyurethane | Apply a coat of stain-blocking primer to keep knots from bleeding through; let dry. |

| PAINTING | CARE | TIP |
| --- | --- | --- |
| For small projects buy 2-ounce bottles of paint or a small can of spray paint. Follow the manufacturer's directions for application of the paint product and for a finish coat. | Follow the paint manufacturer's directions. | Pick up several types of glass paints and try them on inexpensive glass vases to see which type you want to use. |
| Use a primer for nonporous surfaces or an acrylic primer tinted to match the finish color. Roll on two coats of acrylic latex enamel, allowing drying time between coats. Use a 4-inch roller. Make sure to allow extra drying time on humid days. | Protect the surface with a plastic or wood cutting board. Treat gently. Wash with soap and water. Do not use scrubbing compounds. | Countertops get lots of wear, so paint them only as a temporary measure until you can afford to replace them. |
| Prime first even if the directions don't call for primer. Primer always helps the top coat bond better. Shake the can often, and spray lightly holding the can about 10 inches away from the object. It should take several light coats to cover the object. If the spray-coat is too heavy, the paint will run. Allow about 15 minutes of drying time between coats. | Wash as needed. | On a practice piece, try one of the spray paints that goes on without removing rust, and check the piece to see how it stands up outside before using it on your project. |
| Apply a high-quality primer to seal raw plaster. Tint the primer to the color of the wall paint for the best coverage. Paint with two coats of the finish paint. | Wash or scrub—depending on the gloss of the paint—using a mild household detergent. | If you're painting a surface for the first time, always check with your paint retailer about the products you plan to use. |
| Follow manufacturer's directions. Typically, painting several light, even coats, holding the can about 10 inches from the object. Add finishing touches, such as a stamped or stenciled pattern, using outdoor acrylic enamel paint. | Wash with a mild household detergent. | Renew stained and faded outdoor furniture with a can or two of spray paint. |
| Prime the floor using a roller with an extension handle. Paint the finish coat using a high-quality latex or modified epoxy latex paint made for floors (the paint's binder is harder than in wall paint). These paints dry with some give that works perfectly over the vinyl surface. Cover the finished floor with two coats of clear polyurethane. Add an additional top coat of polyurethane every couple of years to ensure durability and cleanability. | Wash with a mild detergent. | Test paint in an inconspicuous area, such as under the refrigerator. To check for durability, let latex paint cure for up to 30 days to duplicate normal household wear on the painted surface. |
| Coat surface with a stain-blocking primer; let dry. Use a self-leveling latex paint in matte, satin, or semigloss for the top coat. In basements, use paint with a mildewcide. | Wash with a mild household detergent. | When painting paneling, use a brush to cover V-grooves and a roller to spread paint over the rest of the surface. Alternate brush and roller so the paint doesn't dry and leave edges. |
| Use a 4- to 6-inch roller to cover flat door panels and cabinet or window framework. Use a brush on molding and rounded edges. Roll or brush in the direction of the wood grain. For added durability on cabinetry, top the paint with two coats of clear polyurethane. | Wash with warm water and a mild household detergent. | Match the primer to the paint, using a water-base primer and polyurethane for a water-base top coat and an alkyd primer for an alkyd top coat. |

# Special paint techniques

| TECHNIQUE | HOW-TO | TOOLS |
|---|---|---|
| **COMBING** | Combing involves dragging a notched comb over a wet glaze/paint top-coat mixture, and removing some of the top coat to expose the satin or semi-gloss base coat color in one continuous motion. This technique can be messy, so protect floors with drop cloths and keep wet rags on hand for quick cleanup. Use the technique on walls, floors, and furniture.  | Combs come ready-made in various shapes and sizes, or cut your own using a squeegee.  |
| **SPONGING** | Sponging produces a soft wall finish using a damp natural sea sponge to apply paint over a lighter or darker base coat. The trick is to use two paints that are similar in color or tone. This technique works especially well on uneven wall surfaces. For added interest sponge stripes or squares rather than the entire wall.  | A natural sea sponge gives the softest finish, but you can also use a sponging mitt or a common household sponge. Experiment to determine the look you like best.  |
| **RAGGING** | Ragging, both positive (ragging glaze/paint mixture on) and negative (ragging glaze/paint mixture off), is one of the easiest techniques. Use a clean, soft cotton cloth to pounce or rub a glaze/paint mixture on or off a painted wall. Use similar colors for a blended look and contrasting colors for a dramatic finish. 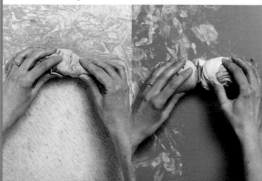 | Sample the look of ragging created using chamois cloth, ragging mitt, paper bag, burlap, and cheesecloth; choose your favorite for your project.  |

| TECHNIQUE | HOW-TO | TOOLS |
|---|---|---|

**DRAGGING**

Create a strié effect by dragging a brush in a long sweeping motion through a wet glaze/paint mixture. The finished effect resembles the texture of fabric. Dragging demands a steady hand for the best results. Wipe excess glaze on a soft rag after each pass of the brush.

A strié brush with stiff bristles produces the best look, but the brush can be expensive. Instead try nontraditional tools such as coarse sponges and wallpaper brushes.

**STAMPING**

Stamp an all-over design on walls, floors, and furniture using a ready-made foam stamp that has been rolled with a thin coat of paint. Press the stamp onto the wall, using even pressure. Carefully lift the stamp from the wall. Because stamps often lack crisp details, the result is a bold graphic treatment.

Special foam stamps, which are larger and easier to hold than smaller rubber stamps used for paper crafts, make embellishing walls and other paintable surfaces quick and easy.

**STENCILING**

Create allover patterns, pretty borders, or random designs using stencils you buy or make yourself. The trick is to invest in the right supplies, such as an adhesive that temporarily adheres the stencil to the surface, brushes and rollers that simplify the painting, and paints that work for this technique.

Stencil crayons, creams, or acrylic paints yield slightly different effects. Experiment to find the look you like best. Shop for stencils online, or in crafts stores and home centers.

# Special paint techniques

| TECHNIQUE | HOW-TO | TOOLS |
|-----------|--------|-------|
| **DOUBLE ROLLER** | Use a special roller and tray for this technique that lets you blend two paint hues to create a soft sponged look. Selecting appropriate colors is a challenge: Too much contrast may give unsatisfactory results, while colors that are too similar may blend too much. | A double roller with sculpted covers lets you apply two shades of paint in one sweep of the roller. These special rollers come packaged with double trays. |
| |  |  |
| **DENIM** | Create the look of denim by applying a paint/glaze mixture on a wall and drawing through the wet glaze to create the look of fabric. A special roller gives the finish the irregular look of woven denim. | A check roller paired with a weaver brush (not shown) gives a denim look to this paint finish. Look for the rollers in home improvement centers and specialty paint stores. |
| |  |  |

# DO THE MATH

Follow these steps to a perfectly patterned wall of stripes, checks, or diamonds.

1. Whether you're creating stripes, checks, or diamonds, you'll need to do a little measuring before you open the paint cans. Get started by measuring the height and width of the walls. Find a number that divides evenly into the wall measurements if you want the design elements to be of equal size. Sketch the walls on graph paper to help you visualize the look.

2. Use a combination level/ruler and colored pencils that blend with the top coat to mark a geometric pattern on the wall. Black pencil lead can be hard to cover up.

3. For a crisp pattern, mark the lines and edge with painter's tape. Re-mark lines as needed to move the pattern across the walls. If you want a painterly look to the geometric pattern, use a level rather than painter's tape to guide your brush without ever letting the paint touch the level. Put painter's tape over the parts of the pattern you do not plan to paint.

TIP: After establishing the first level line, use varying widths of painter's tape to create a striped pattern. Just apply each tape layer adjacent to the previous layer; then remove tape to create stripes.

# SPECIAL PAINTS

The last few years have led to a revolution in paint technology with an ever-growing array of paints. Check out this list for products that are perfect for the projects you're ready to start. Shop your local retailers for other products as well. For a list of manufacturers, see "Sources" on page 186.

• **Chalkboard paint** comes in spray-on and roll-on versions, so you can create write-on surfaces on everything from walls to furniture. Look for spray cans for small projects and buy the paint by the gallon for big projects.

• **Crackle paints** in spray versions make use of a two-step process to create an antiqued finish. Try it on walls and furniture.

• **Denim, canvas, and linen paint kits** let you create the look of fabric on walls and furniture.

• **Fabric paint** can be made by mixing textile medium with any water-base paint. Check crafts stores for 2-ounce bottles of fabric paints.

• **Frosted-glass paint** gives a semitransparent finish to glass objects. This interior paint can make inexpensive glass pieces look expensive. Try it on bathroom windows instead of a curtain.

• **Glass and ceramic paints** offer one-coat coverage on glass and ceramics and are top-shelf dishwasher safe.

• **Glow-in-the-dark paint** lets you create fun accessories for a child's room that glow only after the lights are out. Use it to paint a design on a ceiling or for fun accents.

• **Hammered-metal paint** provides the look of hammered aluminum. Look for these in spray and brush-on versions.

• **Leather-look paint** covers surfaces with the look of suede or leather in spray versions and multistep roll-on products.

• **Magnetic paints** turn any surface into a magnet board. Top the magnetic paint with a fashion paint color.

• **Matte paints** today offer washable surfaces that pair designer looks with easy care. The technology involves mixing ceramic beads with acrylic paint for a finish that is hard and resistant to stains and abrasion.

• **Metallic paints and glazes** add the look of metal leafing and brushed or hammered finishes. Some products are reactive and tarnish over time. Look for metal products available in liquid and spray versions, in sizes from 2 ounces to a gallon, and for interior and exterior applications. Some metallic paints are even safe to use on foam for interior accessories.

• **Mildew-resistant paints** work well in high-moisture interior spaces as well as exterior spaces. They look fresh for years. Some companies offer multiyear guarantees for their products.

• **Mirror paint** gives any clear-glass surface a mirrored look. A clear sealer protects the finish. Look for this product in crafts stores. The product is applied to the back side of glass surfaces.

• **Outdoor paints** in 2-ounce crafts sizes let you embellish metal, terra-cotta, wood, and concrete. Look for these paints in crafts stores.

• **Paint pens** give you the control of a marker with the durability of paint.

• **Paper paints** appeared thanks to the interest in scrapbooking and offer no-warp, acid-free finishes for paper lampshades and more. Look for them in metallic, pearlescent, leather, stone, and stained-glass finishes.

• **Pearlescent paints** top any painted surface with a shimmery look.

• **Plastic spray paint** bonds to plastic without sanding or priming and withstands sun, wind, and rain. Look for these spray paints at home improvement centers.

• **Porch and floor enamels** now come in 1,000-plus colors instead of the limited palette of gray and beige from a few years ago.

• **Stained-glass paint** offers a translucent cover for glass, wood, metal, foil, and paper. This product is acid free and archival safe.

• **Stone-look paints** come in spray-on versions and as kits with multiple steps to create a realistic look.

• **Waterproofing paints** coat unpainted basement concrete-block walls and seal out moisture. Most of these products can be tinted a few basic colors.

# Sources

## CHAPTER 2 COLOR

### P. 14:
Primary chips: Glidden Theatre Lights, That 70's Color, and Sundrenched (yellow); Drum Beat, Victorian Red, and Flaming Sword (red); Rich Navy, Blazer Blue, and Blue Blood (blue).

Secondary chips: Sherwin-Williams Champagne through Marquis Orange (orange); Soothing White through Majestic Purple (purple); White Willow through Espalier (green).

Tertiary chips: Glidden First Light through Jack O'Lantern (yellow-orange); Seashell Pink through Orange Bowl (red-orange); Fleur De Lis through Inkberry (blue-violet); Frosted through Fuchsia Berry (red-violet); Barely Green through Yellow-Green (yellow-green); Aspen Leaf through Blarney Stone (blue-green).

### P. 15:
Complementary chips: Pratt & Lambert Maid of Orleans through Admiral (purple); Lemon Whip through Canary Yellow (yellow).

Analogous chips: Behr Ivory Invitation through Saffron Thread (orange); Moon Mist through Yellow Flash (yellow); Candlelight Yellow through Lemon Grass (green).

Monochromatic chips: Sherwin-Williams Angelic through Rave Red.

### P. 16:
Value chips: Benjamin Moore Crystal Blue through Majestic Blue (blue); Angel Pink through Coral Essence (pink).

Intensity chips: Pratt & Lambert Maid of Orleans through Admiral (purple); Lemon Whip through Canary Yellow (yellow).

Tint chips: Ralph Lauren Makee Island and American Tradition Signature Colors Waverly Home Classics Shadow Blue.

Shade chips: Dutch Boy Plunge Deep through Moon Ridge (brown). PPG Architectural Finishes, Inc. Ash Mist through Bewitched (gray).

## CHAPTER 3 LIVING & DINING

### P. 20-23:
Stencil, shades: Stencil-Ease WP-16, Filligree. Stencil, chair-back: Stencil-Ease CS-17 4-inch lettering stencils. Paint shades: Benjamin Moore Turning Leaf and Berkshire Gray. Trim paint: American Traditions White 44972. Paint, cabinet and chair back: Benjamin Moore Edgecomb Gray. Frames: Krylon Gold Metallic

### P. 24-27:
Wall paint: Benjamin Moore Pear Green and Tequilia Lime. Lampshades and rug: Delta Ceramcoat. Trim: Behr Moon Rise. Black accents: Behr Sorcerer.

### P. 28-29:
Wall paint: Behr Sunporch, Apricot Flower, and Orange Grove.

### P. 30-33:
Wall paint: Olympic Kiwi Splash and Benjamin Moore Ultra Pure White. Paint, fabric shade and pillow: Olympic Turquoise Mist mixed with Delta Ceramcoat Textile Medium.

### P. 34-37:
Paint, walls: Benjamin Moore Artichoke Hearts. Paint, stairway: Benjamin Moore Hydrangea Flower and Delicate Rose. Paint, stencil: Krylon Short Cuts Paint Pen, white. Paint, fabric: Benjamin Moore Hydrangea Flower and Delicate Rose thinned with Delta Ceramcoat Textile Medium. Paint, trim: American Traditions White 44972. Paint, vases: Krylon Frosted Glass Finish 9040 and Pearl Frosted Glass 9044.

### P. 38-39:
Paint, walls: Behr #1A13-4 Buttercorn. Paint, stencil: Behr #W-B-200 Popped Corn and 290B-6 Squash.

## CHAPTER 4 WALLS

### P. 42-43:
Wall paint kit: Ralph Lauren Bright Canvas Morning Pink.

### P. 44-45:
Wall stone finish: McClosky Decorative Effects Textured Stone, Decorative Effects Translucent Color Glaze in Taupe #217405, and Decorative Effects Translucent Color Glaze in Mocha #94825.

### P. 46-47:
Wall suede finish: Ralph Lauren Shadow Ridge SU36 mixed with Tallgrass Prairie SU33 and Desert Cactus SU34.

### P. 48-49:
Paint, ceramic tile: Plaid FolkArt Enamels 4024 Hydrangea and 4019 Fresh Foliage.

### P. 50-51:
Venetian plaster finish: Behr Amalfi Coast VP39 over Behr Shale Gray.

### P. 52-53:
Color-wash finish: Watercolor Walls Moroccan Red and Curry. Stencil: Jan Dressler 681 Elegant Frieze. Stencil paint: Benjamin Moore Audubon Russet and Modern Masters Metal Effects copper paint.

### P. 54-55
Wall paint: Sherwin-Williams Spa #6765. Mural kit: WallNutz Ark Angelz Hippo and Alligator. Mural paints: Delta Ceramcoat Jubilee Green (alligator body), Pumpkin (orange back ridge), Cricket (tummy and stars), Lisa Pink (wings), and Passion (balloon). Mural outline: Painter's paint pen, black.

## CHAPTER 5 KITCHENS & BATHS

### P. 58-61:
Paint, wall, cabinet, and floor: Behr Key Lime, Chilled Lemonade, Soar, and Fresh Water.

### P. 62-63:
Paint, wall: Martha Stewart Signature Color Palette, through The Sherwin-Williams Co. Picket Fence White #8003 and Common Larch Green #8204. Paint, floor: Martha Stewart Signature Color Palette, through The Sherwin-Williams Co. Bluebird #8314. Paint, floor stencils: Martha Stewart Signature Color Palette, through The Sherwin-Williams Co. Blue Hour #8315, Sparkling Brook #8294, and Common Larch Green #8204.

### P. 64-67:
Paint, countertops: American Traditions Obsidian Glass. Paint, cabinets: American Traditions Winter Calm 4001-1B. Paint, floor: Benjamin Moore French Canvas and American Traditions Winter Calm 4001-1B. Paint, shades: Benjamin Moore Turning Leaf and Revere Pewter. Paint, walls: Benjamin Moore French Canvas. Paint, trim: American Traditions White 44972.

### P. 68-69:
Wall, countertop, and cabinet paint: Sherwin-Williams Bayberry SW0103, Regina Mist SW0102, and Porcelain SW0053. Chalkboard paint: Benjamin Moore Chalkboard Paint, black.

### P. 70-71:
Paint, tile: Plaid FolkArt Enamels 932 Calico Red. Paint, wall: Sherwin-Williams Sky High.

P. 72-75:
Paint, cabinetry: The Old-Fashioned Milk Paint Co. Barn Red, Salem Red, and Mustard.

P. 76-77:
Paint, wall: Behr Gulf Stream and Ultra Pure White.

P. 78:
Paint, all surfaces: Sherwin-Williams Divine White, Relaxed Khaki, and Black of Night.

P. 79:
Paint, walls: Krylon Metallic Leafing Silver. Base-Behr Garden Wall.

P. 80:
Paint, walls: Glidden Ocean Voyage. Paint, tiles and wall details: Plaid Folk Art Enamels Sunflower, Berry, Cobalt, and Grass Green.

P. 81:
Seashell stencil: Royal Design Studio. Paint, wall: Behr Hemlock Bud, Spring Hill, and Ultra Pure White.

P. 82-83:
Paint, door: Sherwin-Williams Bravado Red. Paint, wood: Sherwin-Williams Snowbound.

## CHAPTER 6 FLOORS

P. 86-87:
Finish, floor: Minwax Wood Finish oil-base stain in Ipswich Pine #221, and Minwax Polycrylic in semigloss or satin. Stencil paint: Stencil Magic Paint Crème in Pale Yellow and Black Cherry. Stencil: Jan Dressler stencil 699M San Trovaso Medallion.

P. 88-89:
Paint, floor: Sherwin-Williams Great Green and Leap Frog. Stencil paing: Stencil Magic Paint Crème in Snow White. Stencil: Jan Dressler stencil #478.

P. 90-91:
Paint, rug: Behr Bicycle Yellow, Peas In A Pod, Fresh Peaches, Candy Coated, and Ocean Dream.

P. 92-93:
Paint, vinyl: Behr Fairway Mist, Fountain Spout, Pale Daffodil, and Shire Green.

## CHAPTER 7 BEDROOMS

P. 96-99:
Paint, headboard: Benjamin Moore Chalkboard paint in black and Krylon Metallic Leafing KDH5231 Silver. Paint, dresser: Glidden Antique Fresco, Cloud Cover, and Chilly Morning. Paint, chair: Behr Polar Bear.

P. 100-101:
Paint, wall: Behr Glorious Gold and Lemon Sorbet.

P. 102-103:
Paint, wall: Behr Eggnog and Meadow Light.

P. 104-105:
Paint, bedding: Behr Bayou, Shallow Sea, and Pink Punch mixed with Delta Ceramcoat Textile Medium.

P. 106-107:
Paint, wall: Behr Frosted Lemon.

P. 108-109:
Paint, wall: Muralo Scenery Hill, Chili, Sambucca, and Brickle.

P. 110-111:
Paint, wall: Sherwin-Williams Lovable, Amaryllis, and Invigorate.

## CHAPTER 8 FURNITURE

P. 114:
Paint, cabinet: Ralph Lauren Wild Daisy and Design Studio White.

P. 115:
Stencil: Stencil-Ease CS-17 4-inch lettering stencils. Paint, tables: Plaid FolkArt Artists Pigment 503 Yellow Citron and The Old Fashioned Milk Paint Co., Inc. Pitch Black.

P. 116:
Paint, chair: Benjamin Moore Galveston Gray.

P. 117:
Paint, dresser: Benjamin Moore Butterscotch.

P. 118:
Paint, headboard: Benjamin Moore Golden Dunes.

P. 119:
Paint, ottoman: Benjamin Moore Metallic Silver 20.

P. 120:
Stencil, headboard: Stencil-Ease wallpaper and floor stencil WP-11-Pro Damask. Paint, headboard: Plaid FolkArt 320 Jamaican Sea, Delta Ceramcoat Apple Green, and Delta Ceramcoat Soft Grey.

P. 121:
Paint, table base: Krylon Metallic Leafing KDH5230 Gold and Krylon Short Cuts Paint Pen in Gloss Black.

P. 122-123:
Paint, glass tabletop: Krylon Leafing Pen in 9905 Pale Gold and Benjamin Moore Turning Leaf.

## CHAPTER 9 WORK & PLAY

P. 126-127:
Paint, walls: Valspar Decorative Effects Millstone River Shale. Paint, floors: True Value Floor and Porch Paint, white.

P. 128-129:
Paint, walls and floor: Sherwin-Williams Familiar Beige, Domino, and Tanager.

P. 130-133:
Paint, wood paneling: Benjamin Moore Turning Leaf. Paint, brick: Benjamin Moore Ultra Bright White. Paint, concrete-block wall: Benjamin Moore custom. Paint, floor: Benjamin Moore Floor Paint, Light Gray and Medium Gray with stripes of Turning Leaf and Currant Red. Paint, ottoman: Turning Leaf and Red Currant. Paint, lamp shade: Rust-Oleum Silver Hammered Enamel Spray 7213. Paint, desk and chair: Rust-Oleum Silver Hammered Enamel Spray 7213. Pair, chair seat and back: Benjamin Moore Red Currant.

P. 134-135:
Paint, desk: Sherwin-Williams Lime Granita, Exciting Orange, Notable Hue, and Hinting Blue.

P. 136-137:
Paint, wall: Wal-Mart ColorPlace, yellow. Paint, trim: Ralph Lauren Avon Green.

P. 138-141:
Chalkboard paint: Krylon Chalkboard Paint (black) in spray finish. Paint, floor: Sherwin-Williams Sassy Green. Paint, ceiling: True Value Pepper. Paint, pillow: Silver paint pen. Paint, accessories: Plaid Petunia and Kiwi, and Delta Ceramcoat Purple.

## CHAPTER 10 ACCESSORIES

P. 144: :
Paint, chandelier: Krylon General Purpose Metallic in Chrome.

P. 145:
Paint, lamp: Krylon Looking Glass Decorative Mirror-Like Paint.

P. 146:
Paint, basket: Ralph Lauren Jacaranda Pink and Masonry Gray.

P. 147:
Paint, plates: Delta Ceramcoat Mediterranean and Delta Surface Conditioner. Stencil, letters: Stencil Magic 2-inch calligraphy.

P. 148:
Paint, mats: Krylon Looking Glass Decorative Mirror-Like Paint.

P. 149:
Paint, canister: Krylon Pearl Frosted Glass 9044 pearl.

P. 150:
Paint, tablecloth: Benjamin Moore Butterscotch mixed with Delta Ceramcoat Textile Medium. Stamp: Plaid Home Décor 53627.

P. 151:
Paint, lampshades: Krylon Make It Suede! Textured Paint 1241 Buckskin, Krylon Make It Stone Textured Paint 18202 Charcoal Sand, and Krylon General Purpose Metallic 1406 Silver.

P. 152:
Paint, shade: Ralph Lauren Jacaranda Pink and Benjamin Moore Edgecomb Gray.

P. 153:
Paint, plastic urn: Rust-Oleum Silver Hammered Enamel Spray 7213.

P. 154:
Paint, frame: Krylon Premium Metallic 1030 Sterling Silver.

P. 155:
Stamp, pillow: Plaid Décor #53626 Casablanca. Paint, pillow: Delta Ceramcoat Mediterranean mixed with Delta Ceramcoat Textile Medium.

## CHAPTER 11 OUTDOORS

P. 158-161:
Paint, votives: Krylon Frosted Glass Finish in 9044 Pearl Frosted Glass. Paint, chair design: Plaid FolkArt Outdoor Metallic Paint 1642 Silver Sterling. Paint, table: Rust-Oleum Bright Coat Metallic Finish Aluminum 7715.

P. 162-163:
Paint, chair: Behr Cobalt Glaze, Carolina Parakeet, Steam White; Plaid FolkArt Enamel 412 Magenta. Paint, gate: Behr Award Blue.

P. 164-165:
Paint, planter: Krylon Make It Suede! Textured Paint 1241 Buckskin, and Krylon Make It Stone Textured Paint 18202 Charcoal Sand. Paint, sisal: FolkArt Enamels Cobalt 4025. Paint, chair: Rust-Oleum Bright Coat Metallic Finish Aluminum 7715.

P. 166-167:
Paint, concrete: Pittsburgh Paint green 309-7, gold 120-6, orange 125-6, green 209-6, red 231-7, gold 215-4, and plum 438-7.

P. 168-169:
Paint, longue: Krylon Fusion 2439 Satin Pewter Gray. Paint, umbrella: Plaid FolkArt Outdoor Paint 1625 Fresh Foliage. Paint, stencil: Plaid FolkArt Outdoor Paint 1625 Fresh Foliage.

P. 170-171:
Paint, house numbers: Krylon General Purpose Metallic in Chrome and DecoArt So Soft Fabric Paint, black.

## MASTER SOURCES LIST

BEHR AVAILABLE AT HOME DEPOT
800/854-0133 or www.behr.com
Primer, latex and alkyd paint, paint glaze.

BENJAMIN MOORE
800/672-4686 or www.benjaminmoore.com
Primer, latex and alkyd paint, specialty finishes.

DECOART
800/367-3047 or www.decoart.com
Acrylic and stenciling paints, specialty paint finishes.

DELTA TECHNICAL COATINGS
800/423-4135 or www.deltacrafts.com
Acrylic paints, stencils, and foam stamps, including Stencil Magic Paint Crème, Ceramcoat.

DRESSLER STENCIL COMPANY
888/656-4515 or www.dresslerstencils.com
Stencils and stencil supplies.

DUTCH BOY
800/828-5669 or www.dutchboy.com
Primer, latex and alkyd paint, specialty finishes.

GLIDDEN AND ICI PAINTS BRAND
800/454-3336 or www.glidden.com
Primer, latex and alkyd paint, glaze.

KLING MAGNETICS
800/523-9640 or www.kling.com
Magnetic paint.

KRYLON PRODUCTS GROUP
800/832-2541 or www.krylon.com
Primer, spray, chalkboard, plastic, glow-in-the-dark and other specialty paints and finishes, paint pens.

MARTHA STEWART SIGNATURE COLOR PALETTE THROUGH THE SHERWIN-WILLIAMS CO.
800/474-3794 or www.sherwin-williams.com
Latex and alkyd paints.

MODERN MASTERS
800/942-3166 or www.modernmastersinc.com;
Metallic paint finishes and patina-aging solutions.

THE MURALO CO., INC.
800/631-3440 or www.muralo.com
Variety of paint finishes.

PITTSBURGH PAINT
800/441-9695 or www.ppg.com
Primer, latex and alkyd paints, specialty finishes; brands including Pittsburgh Paint, Olympic, Lucite, and Manor Hall.

PLAID ENTERPRISES, INC.
800/842-4197 or www.plaidonline.com.
FolkArt paints for wood, glass, paper, ceramics, and more. Plaid stencils, stencil paints, stamps, and brushes.

PRATT & LAMBERT
800/289-7728 or www.prattandlambert.com
Primer, latex and alkyd paints, specialty finishes.

RALPH LAUREN PAINT
800/379-7656 or www.rlhome.polo.com
Latex paints, specialty finishes, and glazes.

ROYAL DESIGN STUDIO
800/747-9767 or www.royaldesignstudio.com
Stencils and stencil supplies.

RUST-OLEUM CORPORATION
800/553-8444 or www.rust-oleum.com
Primer, spray and other specialty paints and finishes.

SHERWIN-WILLIAMS
800/474-3794 or www.sherwin-williams.com
Primer, latex and alkyd paint, glaze, and specialty paints and tools.

SHUR-LINE
877/748-7546 or www.shurline.com
Paint accessories.

SKIMSTONE
800/444-7833 or www.skimstone.com
Interior concrete paint.

STENCIL EASE
800/334-1776 or www.stencilease.com
Laser-cut stencils and stenciling accessories.

THE OLD-FASHIONED MILK PAINT CO., INC.
978/448-6336 or www.milkpaint.com
Milk paint.

TRU-TEST
773/695-5000 or www.truevaluepaint.com
Primer, latex and alkyd paint, specialty paint tools.

VALSPAR
800/845-9061 or www.valspar.com
Primer, latex and alkyd paint, glazes. Brands include Valspar, American
Tradition, McCloskey, Plasti-Kote, and Laura Ashley.

WALLNUTZ
877/360-3325 or www.wallnutz.com
Paint-by-number mural kits and supplies.

WAL-MART COLORPLACE
800/881-9180 or www.walmart.com
Latex paint.

WATERCOLOR WALLS COLORWASH
866/302-6567 or www.watercolorwalls.com
Color wash kits and coordinating stencils.

WAVERLY PAINT AT LOWE'S HOME IMPROVEMENT WAREHOUSE
www.decorate-waverly.com or www.lowes.com
Interior paints.

# Index

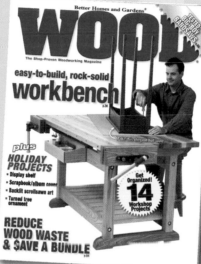